WHAT HAPPENS AFTER DEATH?

You don't have to die to find out.

by STEVEN WEST

in collaboration with Donald Tyburn-Lombard

WHAT HAPPENS AFTER DEATH ® copyright: © by Aabbott McDonnell-Winchester. All rights reserved. Printed in the United States of America by Aabbott McDonnell-Winchester. No part of this book may be used or reproduced in any manner whatsoever without written permission except in the case of brief quotations embodied in critical articles and reviews.

For information, address
Aabbott McDonnell-Winchester Publishers
376 Wyandanch Avenue
North Babylon, New York 11704
(516) 643-3500

ISBN: 0-89519-001-X

© 1977 Aabbott McDonnell-Winchester

Life, as we call it, is nothing but the boundless sea of existence where it comes on soundings.
　　　　HOLMES

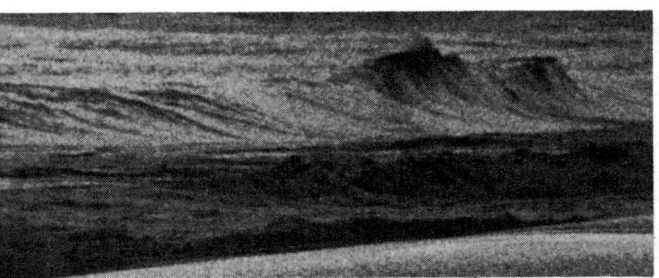

To Sherri

This life, the next life and forever

table of contents

PAGE

AUTHOR'S NOTE 11
INTRODUCTION 13

CHAPTER ONE: THE ORIGIN OF MAN 15
   The impetus supplied by Charles Darwin
   The current theory which evolved into fact
   Consideration of the basic flaw in the theory
   The works of Charles Fort; the denied facts
   The peculiarity of the 'official' mind
   Orson Welles "War Of The Worlds" broadcast
   Australia's 'living' fossil man

CHAPTER TWO:
THE DEVELOPMENTAL
THEORY OF LIFE 29
   The widespread belief in the 'Fall of Man' Concept
   The lack of a central school of thought
   Possibility of a Prime Cause (or God)
   Secondary Causes (or spiritual beings)
   The 'error' that caused them to be cast down
   Multiple lives (reincarnation) to achieve cleansing
   The purpose and meaning of Life

CHAPTER THREE:
THE CONCEPT OF DEATH 37
   Albert Einstein and his two basic theories
   The relation of attitude towards death and vantage point
   Reaction to execution and terminal illness of others
   Freedom through acceptance of death as inevitable
   Acceptance of death in the Animal Kingdom
   Natural and unnatural 'causes' of death views of Man
   Man's continuous fear of the 'unknown'
   Physical death viewed as a natural event
   The difference between personal and physical death

CHAPTER FOUR:
REINCARNATION 53

Persistence in the belief in successive lives
Orpheus and the founding of the orphic religion
The 'Wheel of Life' and the theme of re-birth
Edgar Cayce and his out-of-body experiences
Cayce's first venture into psychic phenomenon
Initial resistance to reincarnation theory by Cayce
Cayce's investigation into thousands of successive lives
Understanding the karmic pattern that governs lives

CHAPTER FIVE:
THE VISIBLE/INVISIBLE WORLD 61

Von Liebnitz and the two kinds of truth
The billion dollar brains employed by science
Discovery of the black 'holes' in space
Reversal of Time within negative space
Disenchantment with the space programs
The real and unreal worlds we live in
Experiments in dimensional 'worlds'
Two, three and four dimensional worlds
Altered beings returning from other dimensions
Ceremonial burial's relation to the invisible world
The significance of the Tibetan Book of the Dead
General Patton at the ancient battleground
Memories and evidence of previous lifetimes
Evidence of life after death; out-of-body experiences
Special case histories of out-of-body experiences

CHAPTER SIX:
THE PSYCHIC WORLD 105

Herodotus, the 'Father of History' explores the world
The oracle and its relation to the psychic world
Mysteries of the brain of modern Man
Primitive Man's investigation of the psychic world
His creation of the half-Man/half-animal god

Primitive Man's journeys to the psychic world
The shaman, the witch-doctor and the ancient priests
The rise to power of the god-kings of Egypt
Amenhotep IV, the heretic pharaoh
Siddhartha Gautama the founder of Buddhism
Jesus of Nazareth and the Nazarenes; Saul of Tarsus
The relentless persecution of the Nazarenes by Saul
Conversion of Saul on the road to Damascus; his error
Ghosts in relation to out-of-body experiences
Famous people who attested to psychic experiences

CHAPTER SEVEN: THE VISITORS/UFO's 125

Dr. Carl Jung and the primordial images of Man
The pattern of images in the mind of Man
Evidence of visitors from other worlds
Erich von Daniken's "Chariots of the Gods"
Walter Cronkites' UFO revelations
Roger K. Temple's "The Sirius Mystery"
Evidence shown by the Dogons of Mali
The mystery of the pyramids of Egypt and Mexico
Technology and the visitors from outer space
Solution of the problems of interstellar space travel
The sudden appearance of Man's larger, altered brain
Man's new ability to 'see' non-existent situations
Extraordinary development of art and culture

CHAPTER EIGHT: MAGIC AND RELIGION 139

Research into the origins of mythology: Grimm's work
The similarity of mythology in all parts of the world
An experiment in panoramic viewing and patterns
Thomas Mann's view of the significance of the myth
The Gilgamesh epic discovered in the palace in Assyria
Early Stone Age Man and the practice of magic
Collection of magic in the caves at Arieges, France
Portrait of the half-Man/half-animal god in the cave
The labrynths and the ceremonial re-birth

CHAPTER NINE:
THE WORLD OF DREAMS 151
The mysterious nature of dreams and dreaming
Ancient and modern theories of dreams
Hippocrates and modern medical thought
Rene Descartes and his: I think, therefore I am.
Continuous activity of the waking/sleeping brain
Psychological disorder caused by dream prevention
Relation of symbols within the body of the dream
Out-of-body experiences opposed to dreaming
Sleeping and dreaming one third of a normal lifetime
The natural and the clairvoyant dream; deja vu
The extraordinary value of the hypnoidal state
The art of remembering all dream details
The censor in the brain and the act of repression
Searching for symbols within the context of dreams
The flaw in the theory of sex symbols by Frued

CHAPTER TEN:
ACHIEVEMENT OF SELF 179
The rise of Earth's great civilizations
The new aristocracy of Knowledge and power
Total power and possession of the priests of Amen-Ra
Toppling of the city-states; twilight of the gods
The new god of science and the priests of science
Sir Isaac Newton and Albert Einstein
Paradox of the altered ape and ultimate technology
Inevitable destiny provided by gods from outer space
The door to the other world in your brain
The ability to move freely between two worlds
Inner knowledge of the truth about yourself
The incredible journey through Time
The ability to create and employ symbols
Re-programming your computer-brain
The initiation of the concept of philosophy
Socrates and the famous socratic method
Aristotle and his creation of logic
The mathematical concept and the basic flaw
The illusion of reality and the disappearance of 'matter'
The sudden memory of a forgotten past lifetime
The shock of recognition of things from the past

CONCLUSION: 211
The summing up.

WHAT HAPPENS AFTER DEATH?

Written by..Steven West
in collaboration with..............Donald Tyburn-Lombard

Graphics Author........................William Alan Discount

Photography by ....Jim Hanson

Research Directors......................................Robert Orgel
................................Sandy Brotman
....................................Beverly Blake

author's note

You are about to read a different kind of book. It differs, in many ways, from anything you have ever read before. The principal difference is that this book is mainly about you. It is deeply concerned with your past, your present life and, most importantly, with the strong possibility that you will have a life after this one. If you can accept that premise, of a life after this one, then please try to accept this simple suggestion. Please try to read this book with an entirely different attitude than the one you might have when you read an ordinary book.

An easy way to achieve that different attitude is to pretend, while reading this book, that you have been selected as a member of a special Grand Jury.

The reason for your selection is based upon the following assumptions:

1. You possess above-average intelligence
2. You are keenly interested in the subject matter
3. You appear to be free of bias or prejudice

As a member of this special jury you will be required to examine and evaluate certain evidence. This evidence may, in light of your previous or current beliefs, distress you. Under ordinary circumstances the nature of this evidence might discourage you from participating in this inquiry.

Please don't let this happen. If you should feel uneasy or distressed, as you begin to view the evidence you are about to be shown, please suspend your final judgement until you have viewed *all* of the material in this presentation.

I can promise you that—to the best of my knowledge all of the evidence is *factual*. If it should be, in any way, speculative or theoretical, I shall say so.

I can also promise you that most of the material will comfort you—some of it may astonish you—but the totality of it will give you new insight into the beauty and magnificence of the life you have now—as well as the life you hope to have.

Steven West
New York, N. Y.
March 1, 1977

introduction

Since the basic premise, that you are a member of a special Grand Jury, has been established, it would seem fit and proper that an opening address be made to you.

The purpose of this address is to acquaint you with the nature of the evidence; the reason why it will be presented in a certain order and, the conclusions that can be derived from the total sum of that evidence.

Ladies and gentlemen of the jury, it is our intention to place before you a body of evidence which, when you have viewed it, will provide you with a total picture of a huge puzzle called: Man, Existence and Death.

The material is arranged in ten separate parts. As you view each part (chapter) you will actually be seeing one part of the huge picture puzzle. As the meaning of that part is made clear to you, the part will fit into place.

Each chapter, then, offers you a part and a place for that part. When the entire presentation is finished, and you have viewed all ten parts, your picture puzzle will be complete and for the first time you will see a total picture of you and your relationship to existence and to death.

It will be obvious to you, at that point, why the material was selected and arranged in a particular way. You will then know the answer to the question that has been posed: WHAT HAPPENS AFTER DEATH?

You will also be able to visit and become familiar with those 'other' dimensions before you 'die' and as a result of that deeper understanding will be able to face death at any time, calmly and without fear.

If you keep those thoughts before you, as you read, you will have little difficulty in understanding the meaning expressed by the material in our total presentation.

Man is a microcosm, or a little world because he is an extract from all the stars and planets of the whole fimament, from the earth and the elements, and so he is their quintessence.

PARACELSUS—*Archidoxies*—1525

chapter 1

the origin of man

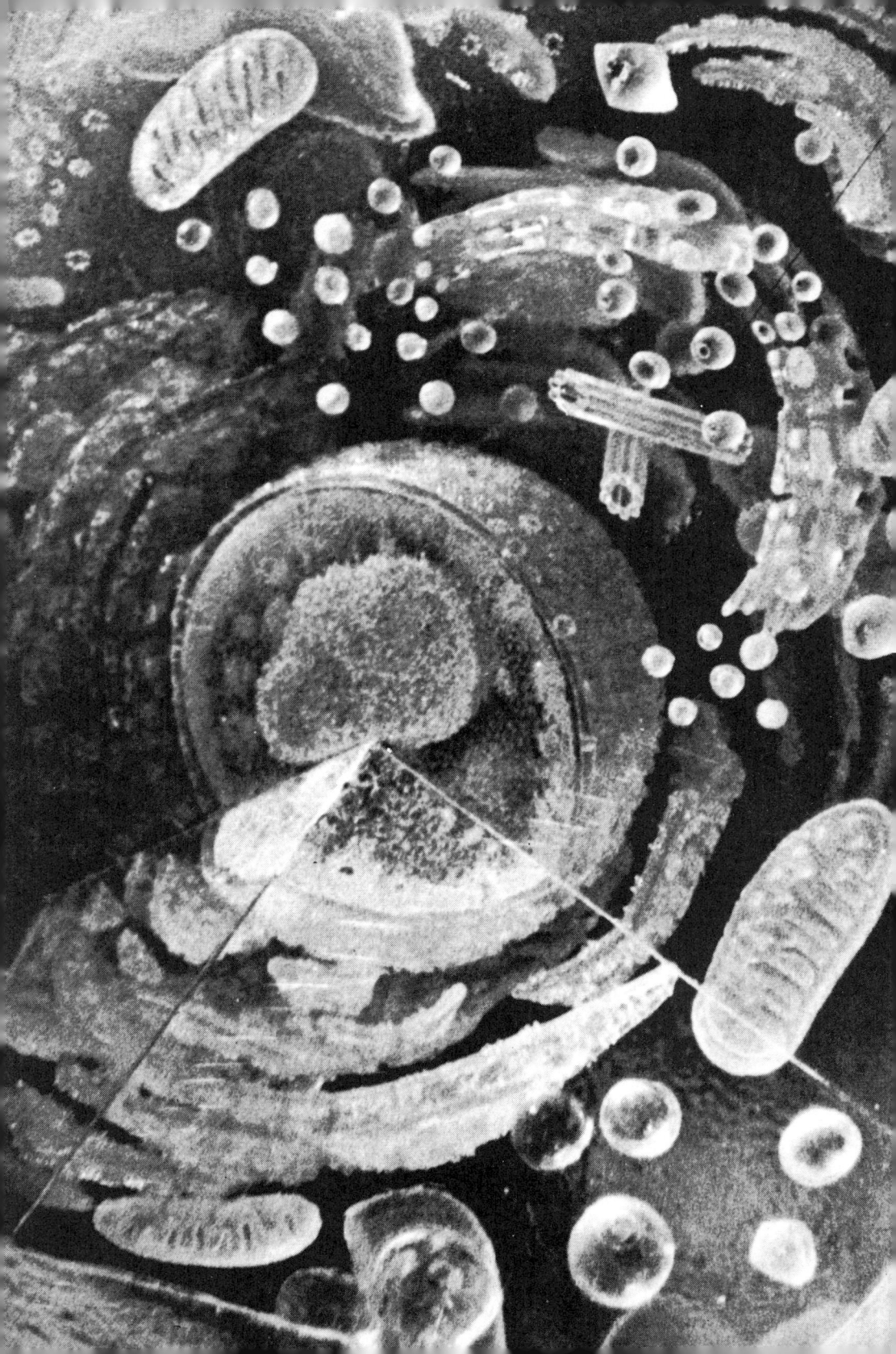

The ultimate forms of existence which we distinguish in our little speck of the universe are, possibly, only two out of infinite varieties of existence.
   HUXLEY

We want, above all, to be fair-minded in the presentation. Obviously, if we presented our side of the case prior to any presentation of the opposing viewpoint, there is the possibility that you might not be inclined toward an impartial attitude.

Let's begin, therefore, with an examination of the current (and apparently accepted) theory as to the origin of Man. This particular theory came into being in 1859 when a naturalist named Charles Robert Darwin first published his essay: "*On The Origin Of Species By Means Of Natural Selection.*"

There were rumblings in the corridors of the scientific community of that era. They were nothing when compared to the violence of the storm that erupted in the hallowed halls of the religious establishment.

Undaunted by this outcry, Darwin then produced an even more provocative essay entitled: *The Descent Of Man*, in which he boldly stated that the human race had evolved from an animal of the anthropoid group.

This was totally unacceptable to churchmen. They attacked both the theory and the theorist by every possible means. At the same time the theory was defended, just as forcefully, by the scientific establishment.

During the nearly six score years since it was first published Darwin's theory has gained almost universal acceptance; not by the Church, of course. They still consider it to be the work of the Devil. You can hardly blame them.

Book publishers, on the other hand, have thrived on this continuous controversy. They have, for almost three decades, produced (usually in time for Christmas buying) large, colorful, expensive-looking, hard-cover books filled with maps, charts and clever artwork. Within the last two decades, large, full-color photographs of bones, skulls, artifacts and location shots of archeologists at work have rounded out these interesting pseudo-scientific books.

The positive assertions of the well-written text and the brilliant supporting photographs offer an inescapable implication that the theory (that Man descended from an ape) is an established, scientific fact.

Is it really a fact?

Let's take a brief look at one of these beautifully bound books. It doesn't matter which one we pick; they're pretty much the same since they all tell the same story. Many use the same photographs. Some of the artwork, however, is original and quite striking.

The first page (after the title page) is usually devoted to a long, impressive list of editorial contributors—the names of highly regarded members of the scientific and educational community—who have written articles for this publication.

Each contributor is listed with all of his college or university degrees (honorary and otherwise) and beneath his name is his professional title.

While the average reader may only glance at this page he has to be slightly intimidated by such a powerful assembly of professionally verified intellect and intelligence.

Upon turning the page, the reader is confronted by a Contents page—usually in large bold letters—which says:

CONTENTS
A PANORAMIC SURVEY OF MAN
AND HIS WORLD

PART ONE: How Man Evolved and Peopled the Earth
PART TWO: Civilizations of Man Since the Beginning
PART THREE: How Man's Ideas Changed the World
PART FOUR: The World Today

You have to be impressed by this kind of statement. You turn the page and usually you are dazzled by a large, full color, two-page spread of a volcano in full eruption. Volcanos are very popular. Most books have at least one.

The real drama begins on the next page which is usually filled with charts, an illustrated scale of life forms and—in the background—a full color photograph of the eternal, rolling sea where, according to the book publishers and contributing editors, all Life began.

The actual story, which begins on the next page, is familiar to you but, in all fairness, we should run through it briefly. In the main, it states:

Our planet Earth began as a mass of hot gas that was almost as hot as the Sun (about 4000 degrees Centrigrade). On or about 5 billion years ago this fiery ball cooled enough to allow the gases to become liquid. At this point, our Earth was a molten liquid ball spinning through space.

When the temperature dropped to 1,500 degrees C a solid crust began to appear at different points. These crusts floated on the molten Earth. At 700 degrees C the crusts were six or seven miles in depth and the cooling rate slowed considerably. A dense cloud formed around the Earth and it began to rain. It rained, we are told, for 60 to 70 thousand years. This constant rain cooled the Earth until it reached something near its present temperature which is 20 to 30 degrees C.

Approximately 3 billion years ago the rain stopped. Earth's atmosphere, at that time, was a mixture of methane, ammonia, carbon dioxide and water vapor.

Earth's crust was buckling, breaking, twisting and folding as huge volcanos erupted almost everywhere.

The vast oceans spilled over the land masses; escaped, were captured by new folds, trapped by new mountains; escaped again and again only to be recaptured at some other point. The entire Earth was a scene of continuous chaos.

Now while all this was taking place hard radiation from the Sun poured down upon the Earth. There were tremendous electrical storms that competed with the fiery thunder of exploding volcanos.

It was these conditions, we are told, which produced a wide range of complex chemicals including amino acids, formic acid and urea. As they formed, they were washed into the oceans where the so called 'soup of life' came into being.

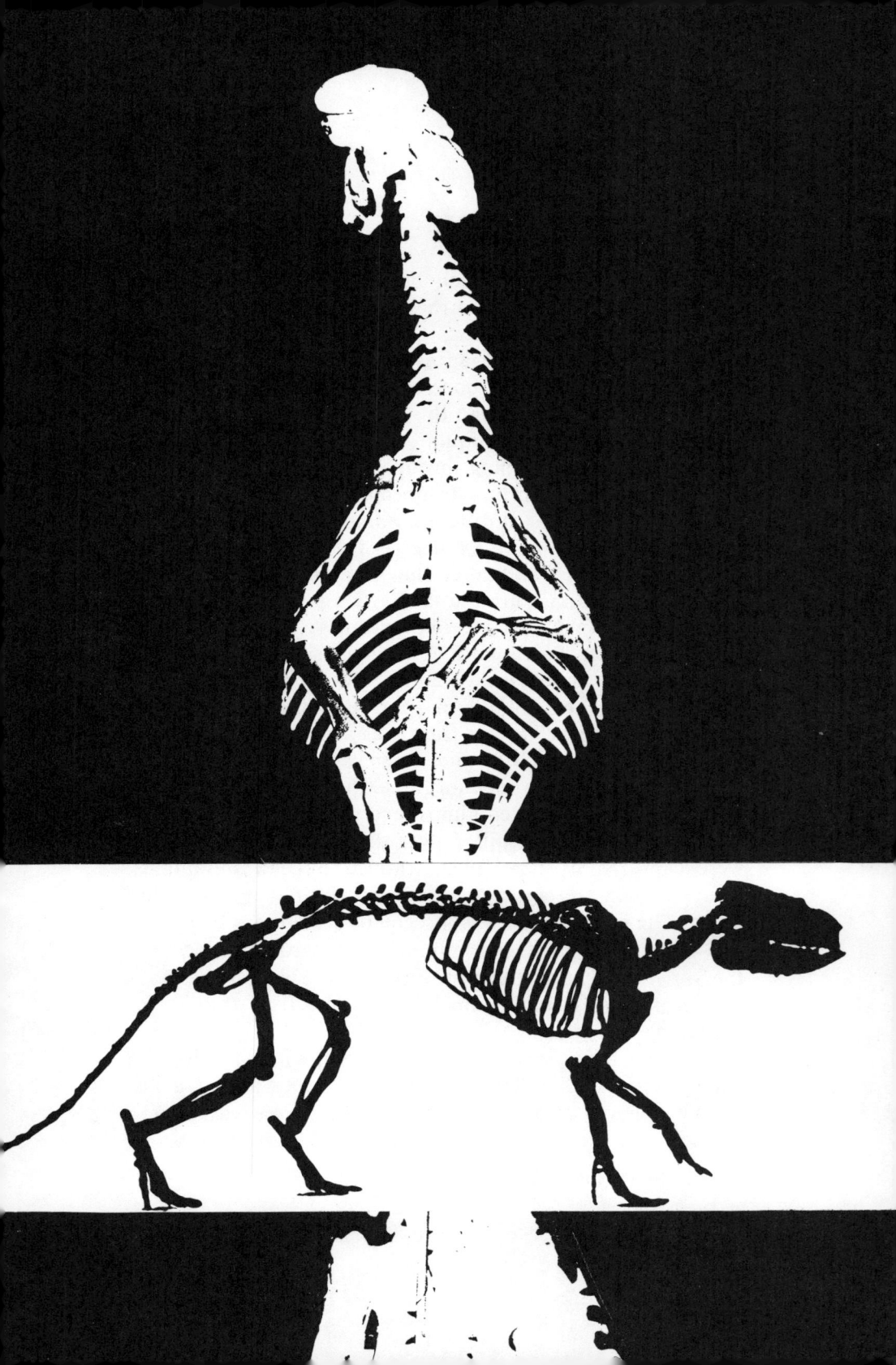

*There were giants
in the earth
in those days.*
    GENESIS

The next stage—which informed authorities label as 'accidental'—was the formation of molecules which, somehow, had the ability to reproduce themselves.

The actual beginning of life—we are told—occurred when a larger, and more complex molecules combined with simpler molecules to form a different kind of structure within a single, reproducible unit. This was the first living cell.

It took these single, living cells about 500 million years to divide themselves into two distinct types—bacteria and algae. These two cells are the foundation cells of all life on our planet. Without them there would be no plant or animal life.

All life forms on Earth were restricted to the oceans up to 500 million years ago. The algae had evolved into plant life forms that were fixed. These in turn evolved into variants of life forms that were not fixed and could move about freely in the sea. These plant forms evolved into primitive fishes and the oceans became thriving communities of life forms.

The next stage of evolution—we are told—began when there was sufficient oxygen in the atmosphere and an ozone layer formed which shielded life forms from hard radiation.

Then the plants came out of the sea and established a firm foothold on the dry land masses. They grew and as they flourished, some of the sea animals began to emerge, first as amphibians and later as reptiles.

These reptiles evolved into the great lizards (dinosaurs) which, for 150 million years, dominated the Earth. Then, about 70 million years ago, something mysterious happened and the dinosaurs were eliminated, almost overnight.

This cleared the way for the emergence of mammals who developed a remarkable number of different types; many surviving to the present day.

The most important of these new types was a primitive monkey-like primate which decided to abandon the plains and the open spaces and live exclusively in the forests.

It was this decision, anthropologists believe, that laid the foundation for the eventual emergence of Mankind. It seems that these furry, four-legged mammals preferred to live in the trees rather than on the forest floor. This tree-life, over a period of millions of years, coupled with the necessity of grasping the limbs of trees, caused the front paws to evolve into a crude approximation of the human hand. This was the beginning.

Twenty-seven million years later, this mammal came down from the trees and began to spend most of his time walking upright. This mammal (named *Ramapithecus*) had almost human hands and, because he walked upright, had greater use of them. He was able to manipulate sticks and stones for simple tasks. He also had a larger brain than his ancestors. He was taller, too. About the size of today's average ape. He managed to survive for about 9 million years.

His successor (*Australopithicus*) was taller, smarter and used the bones of animals and certain stones as tools. He never saved them. He used whatever was handy and then left them behind. Within 2 million years he was smart enough to make tools by striking two rocks together and making flakes.

He was supplanted, 2 million years later by the first true relative of Man (*Homo Erectus*) a tall, straight, smart primate with the ability to make complex tools like hand axes. He was also the first to learn the art of making and using fire.

Two hundred fifty thousand years later the first Man arrived on the scene. *Homo Sapiens* (Thinking Man) with a brain somewhat similar in size and capacity of Modern Man, was capable of making much finer tools with flat surfaces and keen, almost straight edges. A variant of this first Man—*Neanderthal Man*—was a thick, brutish type, less intelligent and less resourceful. It is believed that *Homo Sapiens* eliminated *Neanderthal Man* in the same manner as did explorers in the 15th and 16th centuries who exterminated the primitive peoples they found on the islands they conquered.

The arrival of Modern Man (*Homo Sapiens Sapiens*) or Thinking Thinking Man, took place about 35,000 years ago.

That, in brief, is the current theory of the origin of Man as propounded by book publishers and members of the scientific communities within our modern day society.

It is certainly a most interesting and seemingly plausible theory but is there any solid evidence to support it? There was certainly little evidence to support it at the time that Darwin published his essay: *On The Origin Of Species*—or the later publication of *Descent Of Man*.

Since that time, however, a remarkable number of fossil bones and stone artifacts have been uncovered by archeologists and athropologists in various parts of the world.

Using the carbon-clock (an instrument which determines the amount of radioactivity lost by the carbon in bones and ancient stone tools) has given scientists some idea of the actual age of these artifacts and bones.

If the bones of Man and the tools found near him were of the same Time-period, it was presumed that the tools belonged to the individual represented by the bones. In some cases it was determined that this individual made these tools, as well. The formation of the skulls and the size of the brain pans together with the carbon-clock readings gave anthropologists the 'evidence' of the evolving stages of Mankind.

Now it is readily admitted by most anthropologists that there are many gaps and missing pieces in the chain of evidence they have created. However they maintain that enough evidence has been found to support Darwin's theory that Man did, indeed, evolve from an animal of the anthropoid group.

Perhaps, gentlemen—perhaps.

Why do I say 'perhaps'? Because there is a most serious flaw in this theory. *Early Man is still living in our world.* There is, at this moment, as any visitor to Australia can testify, a large colony of aboriginal men living on that continent. These men resemble, in many ways, that variant of *Homo Sapiens* called—*the Neanderthal Man.*

His size, configuration, skull and his paleolithic (Early Stone Age) culture, confirm this remarkable resemblance to the *Neanderthal Man.*

Why do anthropologists ignore him? Why do they prefer to dig through tons of earth in hope of finding a fragment of a skull, or a shattered thigh bone, when they could be studying this living fossil?

This sub-species of modern Man might have stepped out of the pages of pre-history. He still carries his Stone Age tools. You may, if you wish, watch him *make* those tools on the spot. Why ignore him?

Charles Fort could have given the reason.

This remarkable man spent a lifetime gathering the thousands of facts that scientists choose to ignore because they do not 'fit' the accepted concept of truth; the 'truth' about the world as they saw it.

Charles Fort believed that truth could not be tampered with and still remains truth. It would no longer be the complete—truth—it would be a partial truth and that is as impossible as a 'little bit of pregnancy'—there's no such thing. Fort believed that all of the facts had to be considered before you could arrive at the truth.

A 'fact' in Charles Fort's book was:
(1) Something that had *happened.*
(2) The happening was *witnessed.*
(3) The witness was *reliable.*
(4) The evidence given by the witness was *recorded.*
(5) The recording medium was *reliable.*

Fort took these strict precautions with all of his material because he knew that his book would be under attack as soon as it was published. He was right.

His book documents specific 'happenings' which took place, were witnessed and recorded from 1871 to 1940. They were bizarre, weird, almost inexplicable events and yet—*they are still happening* in many parts ot the world. Every year there are reports of 'strange' things falling from a perfectly clear sky. Manna—for example, that strange, sweet, edible substance which fed the children of Israel as they wandered in the desert.

Blood, bits of flesh, stones, frogs, snails and manna have fallen on the earth from a clear sky for thousands of years. No one knows why or where this material comes from. The 'official' explanation is that this material is 'picked up', becomes part of a cloud formation and then 'rains' down on the earth at some other spot.

That's about as ridiculous as the 'official' explanations given by the U.S. Air Force with regard to UFO sightings by reliable witnesses. For example when an experienced Air Force pilot was killed in a crash while in pursuit of a UFO that had been tracked on radar the official word was: "he obviously confused the planet Venus with a UFO."

Thousands of people, standing in the streets in Washington D.C., witnessed a flight of UFO's over the nation's capitol, The New York Daily News ran a picture of this UFO flight on the front page, and yet the official word was: "*an illusion created by sunlight shining on the windshields of cars.*"

The officials had no comment on the fact that a flight of Air Force planes had been ordered because the UFO flight had been tracked on Air Force radar.

Recently we have heard the 'official' explanation of the strange happenings in the so-called 'Bermuda Triangle'. It's all a coincidence, we are told. There's nothing strange about all those boats, planes and people vanishing in that area.

Why do the authorities take this attitude towards us? Because they believe we are 'children' who cannot be trusted with the truth. We might panic. Justification for this is the 'panic' caused by Orson Welles' radio version of H.G. Wells' novel "The War of the Worlds."

My associate, Donald Tyburn-Lombard, can state from his own knowledge that the reports of the 'panic' were—to say the least—highly exaggerated.

He was in New York City on that particular evening. He heard the broadcast and knew it was entertainment and not an actual news broadcast because at each station break there was an announcement that... "*we will continue with this dramatization of War of the Worlds immediately following these commercial announcements.*"

He states emphatically that the stories about entire communities rushing out into the night and hiding in the woods for fear they would be destroyed by the 'monsters' is pure fiction. It made good 'copy' but it wasn't true.

Yet this is the 'reason' why authorities are afraid to tell us the truth about any 'strange' happening that we might see or come in contact with. Constant official denial, they believe, will make them go away. They won't.

Let us return to further consideration of our living Neanderthal Man. He does exist. No one can deny that fact. Another undeniable fact is that our living fossil has not evolved one inch in 50,000 years. There he sits, in his paleolithic culture, surrounded on all sides by the highly visible culture of Modern Man and yet—he does not evolve.

Something is definitely wrong.

There is something else even more disturbing.

Why, of all the billions of species that have come and gone on this planet, should Man be the only one to 'evolve' to his present unique state of almost god-like development?

This is such an obvious question that you would assume that it has been asked. It has. When we asked a number of distinguished scientists and anthropologists this question we received an astonishing response. The general answer to our question was, "It could have been any other species. It just happened to be Man."

That's not acceptable.

We have every reason to believe that there is another more logical explanation for the extraordinary development of Mankind. We shall not only explore this different explanation we shall also attempt to throw some strong light into the darkest corner of Man's existence and that is—death and what happens after death.

> There wanted yet the master work the end of all yet done; a creature who, not prone and brute as other creatures, but endued with scantity of reason, might erect his stature and upright with front serene govern the rest.
>
> JOHN MILTON—Paradise Lost—1667

chapter 2

the developmental theory of life

We should consider the implications that can be derived from the fact that the majority of people on this planet firmly believe in some form of reincarnation.

It would also be safe to state that the religious groups which have either existed, or still exist, tend to believe in some form of the *concept* of 'the Fall of Man' from a more perfect or 'godlike' state.

These beliefs must certainly be taken into account whenever you attempt to understand your own (and by extension) other people's behavior. In addition you must make certain assumptions as to exactly *what* you are.

These assumptions *might* be derived from any of the many philosophical sources which have been created over the centuries except for the fact that—upon even superficial examination—it becomes quite plain that there is no 'central' school of thought. Philosophers and scholars have been debating and engaging in endless arguments about the correct solution to the three riddles: Where did we come from; where are we now and where are we going when we leave 'here'?

Libraries, usually the best source for factual data, offer little help. They seem to be filled with a sea of contradictory material; a hopeless muddle of beliefs, experiences, opinions, superstitions and prime causes.

The only certainty to be derived from all this material it would seem, is that while philosophers claim to be searching for the truth, in actuality they are really engaged in mounting intellectual attacks upon *rival* philosophies.

If, finally, in exasperation, you turn away from this futile and endless debate and seek the answer within *yourself* it becomes quite obvious that your sensory apparatus—on a conscious level, at least—cannot provide you with the solution to those three riddles.

What then? If you have, at some time during your life, been privy to any one of the many forms of transcendental experience you might be inclined to accept that I shall call, for want of better terminology, Developmental Theory of Life.

This theory simply embraces the belief that, at some unknown point in Time, there was a *Prime Cause* (or God) and there were also *Secondary Causes* (or spiritual beings) and that the relationship between the two was unique since the spiritual beings although they were *derived* of the *Prime Cause* (or God) they were, at the same time, *separate and distinct*.

These spiritual beings, since they were part of the Prime Cause (or God) had God-like powers and also possessed self-determination. At some point, while experimenting with the creation of 'matter' these spiritual beings began to conceive themselves 'greater' than the Prime Cause (or God) and sought to supplant the Prime Cause.

This 'error' caused them to be cast down by the Prime Cause and the spiritual beings were imprisoned in mortal bodies. They were not, however, cast down forever. The spiritual beings could, by means of successive incarnations, through multiple 'lives' eventually emerge cleansed of error restored to a state of grace and be as 'one' with the Prime Cause.

There has been considerable debate as to whether the spiritual beings 'lost' the memory of their former state while inhabiting a mortal body, or whether it was a directive of the Prime Cause.

In any event, the spiritual beings themselves were immortal and would survive the death of their mortal bodies and, somehow, move upward, hopefully, towards a state of grace, with each passing life.

Out of the dusk, a shadow,
  Then a spark;
Out of the cloud, a silence,
  Then a lark;
Out of the heart a rapture,
  Then a pain;
Out of the dead cold ashes,
  Life again.
           TABB

In the periods between incarnation, the spiritual beings would have an opportunity to view and evaluate exactly what they had achieved (or failed to achieve) during the lifetime.

It could be compared to the review and evaluation that takes place, with the aid of films, which professional football teams use to such great advantage. The errors in judgment, as well as the perfectly executed plays, could be seen clearly. The basic object being that each player should attempt to eliminate the 'errors' in the next game.

The spiritual beings would determine the 'cause' of the errors in the past life and hopefully would attempt to eliminate or overcome those 'causes' in the next life they would live.

While there is no certainty that this theory is perfectly valid it does present a 'framework' which can be used effectively in your current lifetime. It could be said that this Developmental Theory:

1. Proposes that personal growth is the major purpose of this lifetime.
2. Offers you a reason for the necessity of failure, suffering and sadness in that these experiences can teach you more than empty 'successes'.
3. Helps you to understand that this lifetime is only *one* of many lifetimes and that while you may not succeed in living it perfectly—it is the effort that counts.
4. Makes 'death' more acceptable because it shows that 'death' is not a finality but rather a 'state' through which your spiritual being passes prior to resuming another life.

Thus, it would appear that the Developmental Theory of Life can be a workable framework because it gives Life some purpose and meaning; it provides you with a direction and it enables you to free yourself from the petty and futile materialism that surrounds you on all sides.

Even if it could be proven that the Developmental Theory is *not* correct—that Life is simply a 'freak' accident—that there is only this life and nothing more—it would still offer, and does offer to many people—a firm foundation for a reasonable, well-ordered and much happier life. If it should work for you, as it does for many people, then it is valid.

If, on the other hand the Developmental Theory is correct, then, in addition to living *this* lifetime to the best of your ability, you will not only have a richer and much more rewarding lifetime, you will have accelerated the elevation of your spiritual being, and shortened the time when you will be reunited with the Prime Cause (or God).

Regardless of whether or not you can accept the validity of the concept embodied in the Developmental Theory of Life you need only ask yourself the simple question:

"Can I accept—as a fact—that there is *no meaning* to this lifetime that I am living?"

You cannot possibly believe that. You cannot possibly believe that all the endless striving of Man for 100,000 years has has been for nothing. That all of Life is, as Shakespeare put it...

"A tale told by an idiot, full of sound and fury, signifying nothing."

You need only look inside yourself, during a quiet period, when there is nothing to distract you, to realize that you are *not* an animal. That there is, inside you, a great font of spiritual belief that has nothing to do with anything you've read, or anything you've been taught; but rather with a knowledge that transcends earthly knowledge.

And what about *death*?

Can you really believe that death is meaningless?

Can you really believe that something as important as death can have no deeper meaning than just extinction? We shall talk about death and its *real* meaning in our next chapter.

No one knows but that death is the greatest of all good to man; yet men fear it, as if they well knew that it was the greatest of evils. Is not this the more reprehensible ignorance, to think that one knows what one does not know?

PLATO—Apology to Socrates 399 B.C.

chapter 3

the concept of death

The subject we are about to explore is death. It is, without a doubt, the strangest of all of the mysteries that surround us because it's the simplest and, at the same time, the most complex phase of our existence.

It could be compared to Einstein's Theory of Relativity. There are less than a dozen living scientists who completely understand Einstein's Special Theory of Relativity. Yet any schoolboy can understand and discuss the General Theory of Relativity. This theory, was written in the simplest form by Einstein and it stems from a childhood recollection of an incident at a railway station.

Einstein, as a mature man, was standing on a railway station platform waiting for a train to arrive when he noticed a small boy, seated at one of the windows of the train on the opposite track.

The train was just starting up and as it did so, the boy leaned out of the window and began to drop pebbles, one by one, on the track below. Einstein was struck by the odd fact that as the pebble dropped from the little boy's hand it described a small arc as it fell. It did not fall straight down. The motion of the train imparted a forward speed to the pebble and so it did not drop straight down as it would have if the train had been standing still.

Einstein suddenly realized that when *he* was a small boy he had also dropped pebbles from the train window and watched them fall to the ground. However the pebbles *appeared* to fall in a straight line.

The sudden realization that any scientist's observation of any physical phenomenon was relative to the location of the scientist's observation point led Einstein towards the creation of one of the most important theories in the history of the world.

Death also has a simple, easily understandable aspect as well as a complex and totally inexplicable one. Then, too, as in relativity, our attitude towards death is determined by the location of our vantage point in relation to death.

Let's see if we can justify that statement.

Let us suppose that you were passing a newstand and you saw a headline on the masthead of one of the newspapers which stated that 500 people were known dead in a South American country as the result of a devastating earthquake. There was a subheadline saying there was fear that the death toll would rise when they started to dig out victims.

What is your initial reaction to that piece of news?

Your reaction has to be impersonal regardless of depth of the compassion or empathy that you are capable of. The 500 deaths you have just read about concerns people far removed from you; people unlike any you know or are familiar with. While you may fleetingly deplore the sad event you will, very shortly, forget all about it.

There's nothing wrong with that. It's perfectly normal behavior on your part. It does not denote coldness or a lack of sympathy on your part. It's just that the incident is too far removed from you and your world.

However, if that headline said 500 deaths had taken place within the state you live in, then your attitude would be entirely different. Death would be a little closer to home. It would concern people very much like you and members of your family. You might even have known some of the victims.

Let's move the catastrophe closer still. Suppose those deaths had taken place in the same community you live in. Now it becomes a much more personal matter and your attitude is drastically different than the one you displayed towards the victims of the South American earthquake.

It's more personal because it could have happened to any member of your family or in your close circle of friends.

Finally, if we move that incident as close as possible and actually involve members of your own family in the death toll, we arrive at the most personal attitude of all.

Now we have involved you in personal loss of a loved one through death. The full weight has now fallen upon you.

Yet, even at this point-blank range, there is one vital element missing—one thing that prevents you from totally understanding the meaning of death. That is the simple and inescapable fact that:

Death is something that happens to someone else.

Now, let's look at another strange aspect of death and that is the subject of 'dying'. This is a totally different concept than death because, even though it is a part of the subject of death it has to do with something that is going to happen rather than something that has already happened.

Again we return to our newspaper headline. You read: **COP-KILLER TO GET CHAIR** and, even though you may agree that the sentence is just and right, there is a slight chill at the thought that a human being is going to be executed coldly, deliberately and methodically.

This is a perfectly natural reaction.

Now let's change the headline slightly.

COP-KILLER DIES TOMORROW

Now your reaction is also slightly different. This human being isn't going to be executed sometime in the future but in a precise number of hours.

Now let's suppose that this 'Cop-Killer' is a member of your family—your son—your husband—your brother—your sister—or your wife.

What is your reaction now to that headline?

To explore still further attitudes, we will continue with the idea of a 'terminal case'. Only, in this regard, we are dealing with death that will be imposed by a *disease* that's incurable. Even though the result (death) will be the same in both instances, the cause of death is different and therefore our attitude must be different.

Again, if we move the frame of reference still closer and suppose that *you* are sitting in the death house awaiting execution—*what do you suppose your attitude would be?* Would it be the same attitude you might have if you were in a hospital bed and had just been informed that *you* were going to die of an incurable disease?

In either case it is safe to state that you would be in a state of shock. There has been sufficient research, in these past few years, to assure us that we have a fairly accurate blueprint of the human reaction to notification of a terminal illness and inevitable death.

At Least 90 Are Killed In **Airline Crash** **Was Strangled**

Killed Driver

Death on a Monday Morning
By ALTON SLAGLE

Testifies Jail Mate Admits Killing Wife **Execution**
By EDWARD KIRKMAN

Slain Youth' Kin Asks

OBITUARIES

Train Kills Girl, 12

2d Fire in a Month Fatal to 2

Apartment House Blaze 2 Men in Bay

DEATH NOTICES

*The certain end of all pain,
and of all capacity to
suffer pain, is death.
Of all the things that
man thinks of as evils,
this is the least.*
        FICHTE

We know each of the stages each person goes through from the original shock reaction—to the outrage and the bitter rejection of the sentence of death—to the bargaining for a postponement—to the deep depression and finally to the acceptance and strange peace of mind that follows.

That description, oddly enough, fits both cases, the criminal condemned to death, and the innocent condemned by disease. The reactions are identical.

What is most strange is that there should be these reactions to the *notification* that you are a terminal case, when the simple fact is, that regardless of your guilt or innocence—regardless of the state of your health or age—*you are a terminal case from the moment you are born.*

You know that you will die. There is no possible way for you to escape the inevitability of your death at some point in your lifespan. Yet you are shocked when you are suddenly notified that you are going to die from execution or disease.

Why?

The answer is quite simple. You have put the thought of your own personal death out of your mind. You have refused to accept the fact that you are mortal. You have lived your life as though you had centuries before you instead of a few years.

Death is something that happens to someone else.

If you have read this far, you are about to make a decision. You are probably saying to yourself,
"I don't think I want to read any more of this."
That, too, is natural.

But don't stop reading now. If you read nothing else in life, what you are reading now is the truth—not only about death—but about *you*.

I can promise you this: If you will face up to your inevitable death *now*—the rest of your life will be richer and more fulfilling than anything you can possibly imagine.

If you can face up to the fact of death it will cease to have power over you. At the moment you do face death and look at it calmly and with full acceptance, the *fear* of death will vanish and never return.

From that moment on, you will be free to live your life fully with enjoyment, *which is the way you are supposed to live.*

Let's place death in its proper perspective.

Death (from any cause) is not a punishment.

If you can accept that simple statement without reservations of any kind then you are free and there is no one in the entire world who can prevent you from being free.

"*The only thing we have to fear, is fear itself.*"

Franklin D. Roosevelt said those words at his inaugural address on March 4, 1933 at a time when this nation, as well as the rest of the world, was floundering hopelessly at the bottom of one of the worst depressions in history.

Those words, and the deeds that followed, helped to bring this nation (and eventually the world) to its feet.

Those words, probably the sanest words ever spoken, should help you to rise from your deepest depression whenever you give in to the fear of death.

Perhaps if we could understand exactly how we arrived at this state of misunderstanding with regard to the true nature of death, then perhaps we would find it easier.

Let's picture a fairly common scene in the African veldt. A mixed herd of gazelles, antelopes and a few zebras are peacefully gathered at a watering hole.

Suddenly one of the gazelles stiffens, raises her head, peers intently at something and then bolts away; and the herd scatters as a charging lion flashes into their midst, captures and kills one of the gazelles and drags it into the bush.

A few moments later the entire herd is back at the water hole, browsing peacefully. The fear is over. The lion has killed and will be satisfied for several hours at least.

All of these animals are aware that death has taken one of their members but that's over and done with.

Another scene: A wounded, obviously dying buffalo is staggering through the brush. It falls, thrashes about, then rises and stumbles forward.

Vultures, at a respectable distance, are following the wounded buffalo patiently. They know he is dying and that it's only a matter of time before he will fall and lie still and then they will dispose of him.

Death acknowledged and death accepted is commonplace in the animal kingdom. We can therefore assume that Early Man reached this primitive understanding of death. He was aware, when one of the members of his tribe was clawed by a leopard or a lion, that death could follow rapidly.

He could also understand that if a member of his tribe fell from a high place, death could follow. He could easily understand that death almost always resulted from deliberate or accidental violence.

BECKIE
1931 — 1946

OUR BELOVED DARLING

CINDERELLA
1945 — 1955

EMILY
1948 — 1962

POLLOCK

BABY THANK YOU FOR ALL
THE JOY YOU GAVE US
ALL OUR LOVE

This was natural. This was simple 'cause and effect'.

However he was baffled by death that was not caused by *visible* violence. Death from disease was completely beyond his understanding. Death from shock—from heart failure—from a thousand invisible sources—was incomprehensible.

Man, in his later stages of development, still suffered from the same inability to understand that death was a *natural* event. However, as Man progressed, he began to fashion *reasons* for these mysterious deaths. And those reasons, with variations have persisted right up to the Twentieth Century.

Let's examine some of these beliefs for a moment.

Death is only natural if you can see exactly what caused the death. If you cannot *see* the agency or cause then death is unnatural and is therefore the work of a sorcerer, a witch, or a malicious spirit. In some cases it could also be ascribed to an 'angry god'. The god depended on the location of the death.

They did not know that disease existed, nor were they aware that certain diseases could cause swelling and rotting of the limbs (Hansen's Disease or leprosy). Death, in this manner, was obviously the work of demons.

It's difficult to believe that this kind of ignorance could possibly exist in this current Age of Science but it does, in a great many countries around the world, and even here at home, in these enlightened United States.

So we shouldn't find it difficult to understand that Man had to blame *something* for these mysterious deaths. He created the 'supernatural' and was satisfied with that explanation—satisfied for a long time, evidently because we still have people who believe in the supernatural.

There is no supernatural.

There is only natural cause and effect.

There are no 'witches' (in the magical sense) no sorcerers, no demons, no devils (with big or little "D") and there is no such thing as 'possession' much as the movie-makers would like you to believe that there is.

There is only truth and falsehood; real and unreal; knowledge and superstition.

And the truth shall set you free.

The vast majority of people in this world never have been free. Whatever freedom they thought they possessed were just as mythical as their ideas about the supernatural.

No one can be free so long as he is enslaved by a falsehood. To believe that death is a punishment is to permit yourself to be enslaved by the fear of that punishment.

Man to the present day fears what he cannot explain.

Since no one (to my knowledge) has ever given Man a satisfactory explanation of death—Man naturally fears death.

A philosopher named *Epicurus* made an interesting observation around 300 B.C. He said,

"*Death, feared as the most awful of evils, is really nothing, for so long as we* are, *death has not come, and when it comes, we are* not.

Now that is a clever piece of reasoning but it does not give us the kind of explanation we deserve.

What is wanted is a piece of wisdom that is simple enough to understand and sound enough for us to accept.

> *Michel De Montaigne,* the noble essayist said,
> *"If I were a writer of books I would compile a register, with a commentary, of the different deaths that men die, for he who would teach men how to die would also teach them how to live."*

Now *that* is much closer to the mark, but still not close enough to satisfy our requirements.

Francis Bacon, in his essays in 1597, said,

> *"It is as natural to die as to be born."*

And that is exactly the point.

Death is a natural consequence of life. If we imagine death to be an evil thing we distort what is probably the most natural and most valuable asset of life.

> Life and death makes a perfectly balanced equation.
> Life without death is a meaningless equation.

Let's try to imagine what life without death might mean. I mean that you should think of eternal life, and what it would be like if it were impossible to die. You had to live forever—for eternity. There would never be an end to the life you are now living. Think about that, for a moment and while you do, remember these sage words:

> *"It is amusing to realize that there are millions of people yearning for immortality—and these same millions are the people who don't know what to do with themselves on a rainy Sunday afternoon."*

Can you honestly say that you think it would be a boon to be told that you were going to live your present life forever—to the end of Time?

No, you would not, because it is death that gives meaning to life. It is the fact that we have a finite piece of time in which to live that gives character to our deeds, gives meaning to our acts of heroism or self-sacrifice for another.

Have you ever wondered why there is no other definition of death than: *the cessation of life or life functions*? This is the *only definition possible*.

It has been said that men fear death because they fear a *personal* death—or a death of *themselves*.

The self does not die—the body dies. The self is eternal.

Take the philosophers I have quoted in this chapter. Their bodies have been dead for centuries but their minds are alive. When I sit and read the work of these ancient thinkers it is their minds that speak to me across the gulf of years. They teach me wisdom as surely as if I sat at their feet or walked with them through the olive trees in the hot sun.

They are not dead. Their bodies are dead.

Just as my body may be dead as you are reading these words, but my mind is alive and speaking to you. Thus the essence of me still lives and works for what I believe in. The essence of my thoughts are still here.

I cannot sum it all up better than this old friend did, in 40 B.C. in his Astronomica I.

> *"No barriers, no masses of matter however enormous, can withstand the powers of the mind; the remotest corners yield to them; all things succumb; the very Heaven itself is laid open.*
>   MARCUS MANILIUS

Death cannot be construed as an exit from life, but as an entrance to a higher plane of existence which the essential being will occupy for a period of rest and then, at a later date, your being will reenter this lower plane of existence and begin again the task of leading still another life. Hopefully a better life than the one you lived previously because your essential being will have learned something in that previous life and will not repeat the errors but rather tend towards living a more perfect, richer and more rewarding life.

With that thought in mind let's examine some of the aspects of one of the oldest beliefs of Man.

All things return eternally and ourselves with them; we have already existed times without number and all things with us.

NIETZSCHE—
"Thus Spake Zarathustra"

chapter 4

reincarnation

Belief in the theory of reincarnation—that Man is a spiritual being who uses a mortal body like a garment which he sheds at death only to take it on again in a successive life—has *persisted*, as far as we know, for as long as Man has been capable of *thinking*. Even before the advent of writing, Man was expressing this concept in song and ritual.

Continual reference to the concept of reincarnation in one form or another—with names that include such terms as palingenesis, metempsychosis, transmigration—has been uncovered by archeologists in the written or carved expressions of every civilization of Man.

Orpheus, the legendary founder of the Orphic religion which flourished in ancient Thrace, is said to have stated that the 'soul' and body of Man were united in a special kind of 'compact' wherein the 'soul' being divine and immortal, continually struggled to free itself from its mortal prison.

Only 'death' could dissolve the 'compact' and permit the soul to fly free. The freedom was short lived because shortly thereafter it was recaptured and imprisoned again in another mortal body. The 'wheel' of birth and rebirth rolled on inexorably to the end of all Time.

It is interesting to note that the 'wheel' of birth and rebirth is a recurring theme in many Eastern religions and philosophies. The Tibetans refer to the great 'wheel' that rolls through Sangsara (the world) bearing with it the soul and body of Man together with gods, devils and yiddags (demons). Again, in the great ruins of Angor Wat in Cambodia may be seen the gigantic sculptured 'wheel' erected by the members of that vanished, ancient civilization. Our modern reference to the 'wheel of fortune' contains an echo of this ancient concept.

The ancient Egyptians—with their legend of Osiris and his rebirth—and the subsequent theory of reincarnation which led them to preserve the actual body so that it could be used again—is certainly a familiar story.

The earliest Greek thinker who has been connected to the concept of reincarnation is Pherecydes, the teacher of Pythagoras who, in addition to laying the foundation of geometry, also founded a religious sect (the Pythagoreans) who espoused a concept of reincarnation similar to that propounded by Orpheus.

The concept and the belief in reincarnation has passed down through the endless centuries to the present day.

While belief in reincarnation has been publicly expressed by many of the world's most notable figures it wasn't until the emergence of Edgar Cayce in 1910 that we began to receive direct and positive proof of the existence of a world beyond this and the 'river of knowledge' that it contained.

Edgar Cayce, a man with no more than a seventh grade education, could, while in a self-induced hypnotic state, give a perfect medical diagnosis of any patient without ever seeing the patient in the flesh. Doctors merely had to give him the name and address of the particular patient and somehow Edgar Cayce was able leave his body (out-of-body experience) go directly to the body of the patient—enter it with his mind—explore it—and then, while still in his hypnotic state dictate the complete details of the illness or disease. He could go further. He could also *prescribe* the treatment. A number of physicians in Kentucky used Edgar Cayce's extraordinary talents and one of them, Dr. Wesley Ketchum submitted a report of these

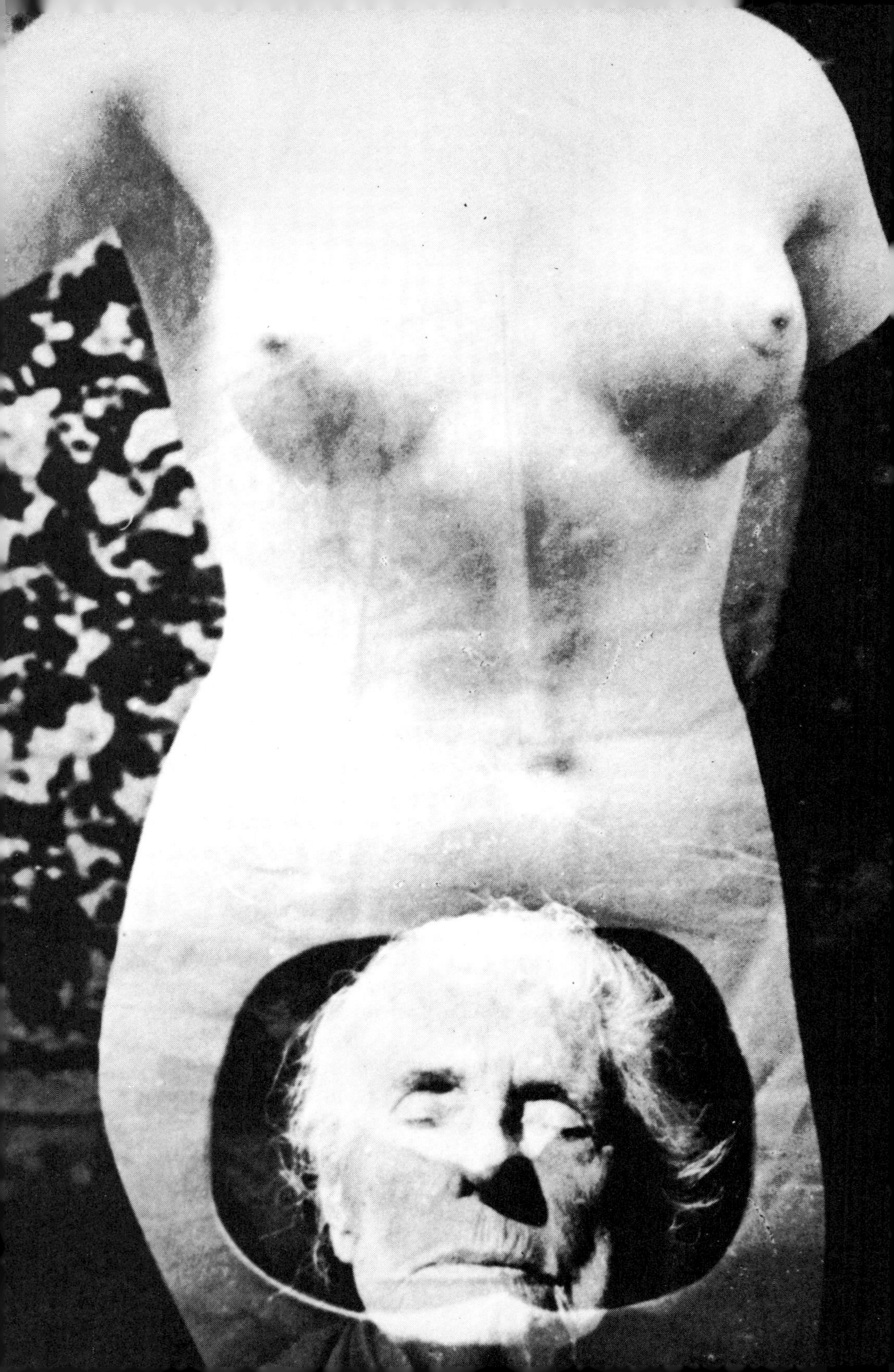

*Revelations
explains all
mysteries except
her own.*
  COWPER

astonishingly accurate diagnosis/treatment dictations to a research society in Boston. Subsequently The New York Times carried the story and from that day (October 9, 1910) until January 3, 1945, when he died, Edgar Cayce's extraordinary talents helped thousands of people to overcome disease.

We are not as concerned with Edgar Cayce's unique medical talents as we are with the *other* aspects of his extraordinary capabilities.

That is his penetration into and his ability to perceive the *past* lives of people who sought his help with their psychological problems rather than physical ones.

According to Edgar Cayce's son, Hugh Lynn Cayce, his father was a devout and orthodox Protestant who was shocked and dismayed to learn that, while in his self-imposed hypnotic state, he had clearly stated that reincarnation was not a myth.

The incident, which was to have far reaching effect upon the thought and teaching relative to psychic research for the next half century, took place on August 10, 1923 in a hotel room in Dayton, Ohio.

Although Edgar Cayce had been diagnosing and helping to cure physical ailments for more than 20 years he had never, until that moment, ever been asked to investigate the area of psychic phenomenon.

The man who instituted the investigation, Arthur Lammers, was a serious student of psychic phenomena and Eastern religion at a time when such activities were considered disreputable to say the least.

Cayce was, according to all accounts, completely repulsed by the notion that Man had the ability to live more than one life as a human on Earth.

To him, such an idea was sacrilege and completely at odds with his conscious Christian belief. He refused, at first, to believe that he could possibly have defended the concept of reincarnation but the stenographic report of his statements—the obvious integrity of the people with whom he was working—at last convinced him to explore further into this strange and disturbing region.

In the years that followed, Edgar Cayce was to give complete and detailed descriptions of *previous* lives to more than two thousand people. His descriptions also contained the 'errors' of the previous lives as well as the 'good and natural' inclinations of the soul.

These 'readings' with their recommendations for certain conduct in this present life, when followed, led to many startling successes for these people.

One of the most interesting was that of a young man with little or no prospect for the future and seemingly little talent. Cayce traced back his previous lives to a point more than 10,000 years in the past. It was a truly astonishing 'reading' rich in historical accuracy but even more importantly it uncovered certain 'traits' and hidden talents in the young man.

The full account may be found in Noel Langley's excellent book: *Edgar Cayce on Reincarnation* published by Warner Paperback Library.

The end result of this particular reading was—that even though the young man was reluctant to follow the recommendations Cayce gave him—he eventually tried and ultimately succeeded—exactly the way Cayce had predicted—and needless to say became a fervent admirer and worked closely with Edgar Cayce until the latter's death in 1945.

It was Cayce's belief that vocational failures, mental 'blocks', erratic behavior, self-destructive tendencies and other psychological disorders could only be understood in relation to 'karmic patterns' which had been established during the 'previous' lives a soul has lived on Earth.

Karma was, in his opinion, a universal law of cause and effect which governs the actions of a soul each time it enters the Earth-plane as a human. While the soul has complete access to all of the characteristics, mental capacities and skills it acquired in previous lifetimes, it must also bear the brunt of the corrosive effects of lives in which negative actions took place involving greed, hate, cruelty, lust and meanness of spirit.

The 'negative' aspects are burdens which must be 'worked off' during successive lifetimes. It is these 'karmic burdens' which help to explain much of the apparently 'needless' suffering of the 'innocent' such as children born with a crippling defect; or 'good' people who suffer misfortune.

The advent of World War II and the ensuing chaos obscured the final days of Edgar Cayce but interest in his work was rekindled with the emergence of the astonishing book *The Search For Bridey Murphy* which caused a wave of controversy in the mid-fifties.

This remarkable, recorded account of a woman who described, in considerable detail, the previous lives she had lived produced a wave of interest in reincarnation.

We have, since that time, seen a steadily increasing amount of material dealing with evidence that most of us have lived previous lives. It would seem than, that not only *is there another life after death* but there is a *succession* of lives after death to be expected.

In our next chapter we are going to examine some of the aspects of this 'other- dimension we may expect to enter, temporarily after our 'death'.

This world, after all our science and sciences, is still a miracle; wonderful, inscrutable, magical and more, to whomsoever will think of it.

THOMAS CARLYLE—1840

chapter 5

the visible world

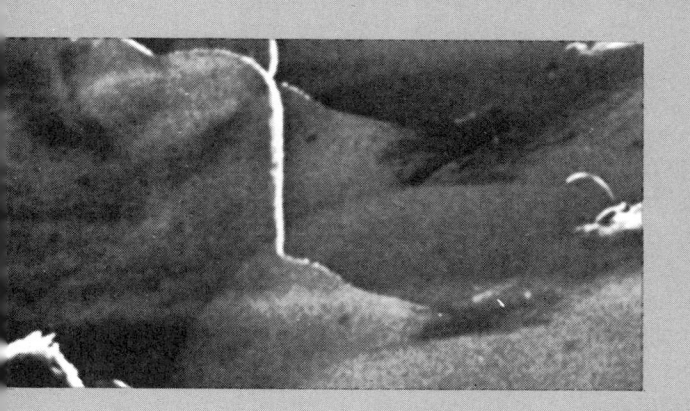

and the invisible

Truth is a strange commodity. There is a noble ringing sound whenever we pronounce the word aloud. Somehow, whenever we manage to tell the truth we feel a mantle of virtue settle over us; or possibly there is the relief and brief luxury of the absolution which follows our admissions in the semi-darkness of the confessional.

Truth, however, is neither singular nor absolute. Baron Gottfried Wilhelm von Leibnitz, the German philosopher and mathematician believed that...

"There are two kinds of truths; those of reasoning and those of fact. The truths of reasoning are necessary and their opposite is impossible; the truths of fact are contingent and their opposite is possible."
The Monadology, XXXIII, 1714

What we are going to deal with, in this chapter, is the truth about the world you are living in; a world that is composed of visible and invisible parts.

Our scientists believe that they are well on the way towards discovering the truth about the nature of the world we live in and—it would seem—they may be right.

According to these worthy and noble seekers of the truth, we are standing on the threshold of the greatest 'information-explosion' in the history of Mankind.

The giant computers, the 'billion-dollar-brains' of Earth's vast scientific community, are humming, whirling, winking and hissing happily in this last quarter of the Twentieth Century. Thanks to the host of new, sophisticated, electronic information-gathering devices that have been created in this Age of Space, endless streams of facts and figures are flowing into the enormous memory-banks of these huge, man-made imitations of the human brain.

The contents of this river of knowledge range from items as simple as the nature of tomorrow's weather to a subject as complex and mysterious as the 'black holes' in space.

Scientists believe that these 'black holes' are the residue of ancient suns which exploded and then collapsed into a *reversal* of being or—to put it another way—became the *negative* state of what had been *positive*.

Under such conditions, they believe, Time would be *reversed* inside one of these 'black holes' and it has been suggested that a spaceship which entered this negative space would be thrust backwards, at the speed of light, to the beginning of Time.

One bright young scientist, after listening to this theory, suggested that a remote-controlled spaceship equipped with television cameras, be sent into one of these 'black holes'. This, would record the reversal of Time on videotape.

An older scientist pointed out the possibility that, since both the spaceship and television cameras were, in essence, products of Time, they would also be subjected to the reversal effect and would ultimately disappear.

This is heady stuff, particularly when presented to science-fiction buffs who thrive on this sort of speculative thinking and seem to regard scientists as a breed apart possessed of almost god-like insight into the mysteries which surround us on all sides.

You, on the other hand, may not share this enthusiasm and may well deplore the multi-billion-dollar rockhunting expedition to the Moon or the sand-siphoning activities on Mars. You may ask questions concerning the validity of the reasoning which has prompted these incredibly expensive excursions. You might, for example, suggest that you are more interested in the nature of the invisible world you are living in *at this moment* than you are in the nature of the universe 5 or 10 billion years ago.

Space and time, and with them all phenomena, are not things by themselves but representations, and cannot exist outside the mind.
KANT

It is quite possible that you eventually became bored with the Apollo Space Program and that you did not take as great an interest in the last few voyages to the Moon as you did in the *first* of the Apollo missions.

You may have felt a faint tinge of 'guilt' when an acquaintance asked if you had watched the last mission on television. Perhaps you winced when you heard some of the harsh statements made by august members of our scientific community who lashed out at your lack of interest in what they termed: "The greatest scientific achievement in history."

You were, as I seem to recall, roundly criticized for your lack of interest in the latest 'up-to-the-minute' report on 'our men in space'.

The fact of the matter is—it was the *scientists* who were being childish. They were pouting and sulking because we were not paying enough attention to the wonderful things they were doing with the multi-billion-dollar 'toys' we gave them.

They were right. We were *not* paying attention because it became obvious that the only result of this enormously expensive program was to *confirm* certain 'scientific facts' obtained many years before by mathematical calculation.

If—instead of spending those billions of dollars in a futile exploration of the *physical* world—the same amount of money, time and effort had been spent in securing and analyzing data about our *non-physical* world we might have gained considerable insight into those twin-mysteries which concern all of us—*life* and *death*.

No one will deny that life and death are unsolved mysteries. Another undeniable fact—despite the Niagara of knowledge that has poured into their giant computers—is that 'scientists' are no closer to the truth than Aristotle was in 322 B.C.

Let's examine certain aspects of our 'visible' and 'invisible' world and see exactly why it's so difficult to uncover the 'truth' about each of them.

The 'invisible' world we are speaking of is *not,* for example, the microscopic and sub-microscopic aspect of our world which may only be viewed with the aid of an optical or electron microscope. Nor are we speaking of the macroscopic aspect viewed with an optical or radio telescope.

We are speaking of the 'invisible world' that is a vital part of our 'visible world'. A world that surrounds us every moment of our life. It is a *real* world, of vital importance to us, and yet— we can neither 'see' it, nor can we fully understand it.

Yet we *must* understand this world if we are to make any sense at all out of the 'life' we spend here on Earth.

The reason we find it difficult to 'see' this *real* world is because we suffer what I will call *dimensional blindness*. This can be understood, if you will perform a simple experiment.

Look at the page of this book you are reading right now. It has three dimensions—length, width and some slight depth (the *thickness* of the page). For our purposes we shall pretend that this thickness does *not* exist.

We therefore have a perfectly flat, two-dimensional surface. Let's call this a 'two-dimensional' *world*.

Let us further suppose that the *letters* of the words on this page are *people* who inhabit this two-dimensional world.

Now we have a 'world' in which 'people' cannot 'see' *depth*. They are completely unaware that depth *exists*. These two-dimensional 'people' can move right, left, straight ahead or in circles but they cannot move 'up or down' because, for them, *up or down* does not exist in their world.

Nor are they aware that *you*—from your lofty *three-dimensional* vantage point—*exist* and are watching them as they go about their daily lives.

Now we shall try the first of two experiments.

Place one fingertip gently into the center of this two-dimensional world you have created.

What do you suppose the reaction will be to this sudden and 'mysterious' intrusion into their little world?

Since these two-dimensional beings cannot 'see' depth they will only be aware that some kind of a 'force' has appeared which blocks their efforts to move in a straight line but permits them to go *around* this peculiar barrier.

'Scientists' in that flat little world will, of course, offer a 'logical' explanation and talk glibly about sun-spots 'force-fields' and the like; but not even the most brilliant mind in that entire world would be able to conceive that this circular 'force-field' is actually the tip of an enormous finger.

Nor would that being be able to understand that the finger belonged to an enormous, intelligent being that was, at that moment, observing the reaction of their people to the intrusion of that finger.

Now let's perform another experiment. Let us suppose that you could reach into this world and remove one of its citizens. No one would see this action. One moment he would be visible and the next moment 'invisible' as you lifted him into the third-dimension. If anyone in that little world 'saw' the vanishing act he would tend to disbelieve it because it was 'impossible'—that he was suffering from an hallucination.

Now that you have removed this citizen, you then endow him with the ability to 'see' depth and permit him to observe your three-dimensional world *as well as his own flat world.*

You then return him to his world with his memory intact so that he is fully aware of what he has seen and experienced during his excursion into your world.

Can you think of any way in which this 'altered' being could possibly describe his experience to his fellow beings so that they could understand exactly what had happened to him?

Now let's try a variation of that experiment. *You* are a three-dimensional being living in what appears to be a three-dimensional world. You have no ability to 'see' another dimension therefore, there *is* no other dimension.

Suppose, for the moment, that there *is* another dimension and suppose that there *is* a four-dimensional observing *you* in your world just as you observed the little two-dimensional being in his little world.

Let us further suppose that this four-dimensional being plucks you from your world—gives you the ability to 'see' that extra dimension—and then returns you to your world with your memory intact.

Do you suppose that you could tell anyone exactly what happened to you with any hope of being understood?

There is one other factor of importance. You would have been *altered* by that experience. You would now be able to 'see' that extra dimension. That knowledge would change your outlook on life completely. You would be a different kind of person from that point on. You would, in essence, be a man with one eye in a world of blind men.

Is there any evidence that this kind of dimensional experience has happened to Man? There is a great deal. Not just in recent years but at the beginning of Man's existence.

Let's move back in Time to the year 1857. In that year, anthropologists discovered the remains of a 70,000 year old Neanderthal Man, in a cave in the Neander Valley near the city of Dusseldorf, Germany. This was the first species of Man (as far as we know) to engage in ceremonial burial instead of simply abandoning his dead to the vultures.

It's beginning of the belief in life after death.

Where could that belief have come from unless from a journey to the 'other' dimension and the return in an altered state. In his primitive state it was difficult to communicate what had happened and so ceremonial burial was the form the communication took.

The ancient Tibetans created an astonishing work which has been aptly named: The Tibetan Book Of The Dead by the scholars who discovered it. This unique work has also been called a 'traveler's guide to the other world' because it gives a step-by-step description of exactly what happens from the moment of death until the moment of reincarnation some 49 days later. It was designed by the ancient lamas as a course of instruction in the 'art of dying' for the novitiates who entered the lamasery. It described, in considerable detail, the different dimensions the spirit (soul) of the dead would pass through during the 'journey between lives'.

The same set of instructions were given again to the dying, to prepare them for the journey they were about to undertake. The hope was, that during this journey, the spirit (soul) could reach sufficient enlightenment to reach and join the ultimate being (godhead) freed of the necessity to reincarnate.

The Egyptians too, had a Book Of The Dead, but rather than manuscript, it was painted or carved in the walls of the tombs for the dead. It consisted of a series of panels which showed the passage of the ka (soul) through the many trials that would take place before the ultimate trial wherein the heart would be weighed on a scale against the 'feather of truth'.

Unlike the Tibetans who believed the reincarnation would be a 'new' life in a new body—the Egyptians believed that the dead would come back to occupy their own body. This is why they embalmed and preserved the bodies of the dead.

These two remarkable works, separated by thousands of years and thousands of miles had to be produced, originally by altered beings who were attempting to explain, as best they could, exactly what happened after death.

So now we have a chain of action, spreading across some 70,000 years, which clearly shows that Man had a strong *belief* that there was a life beyond this one.

Belief, in itself, is *not* evidence. It might be no more than wishful thinking. What we are looking for is evidence that *you* have lived before. Evidence that shows that you have lived countless lives in the past and will live countless future lives.

Is there any evidence of this?

Yes. There is.

Do you remember, in the motion picture PATTON when General Patton asked his jeep-driver to stop at that ancient battleground in Africa. Do you remember how he described the ancient battle and then said, "I was *here!*"

He was right. He was there, and took part in that battle, a thousand lifetimes ago.

The proof that we have the extraordinary ability to live successive lives has been with us almost from the very beginning. Let's examine a few of the many thousands of pieces of evidence that exist.

There have been repeated instances, which have been recorded, from ancient times right up to the present day, of the extraordinary abilities displayed by extremely young children. Abilities that cannot be accounted for by a high order of intelligence or inherited characteristics.

An infant of three years of age suddenly, without instruction of any kind, begins to compose brilliant and complex pieces of music. Now you should understand that music is composed in a particular, unique *language*. It also consists of certain mathematical formulas and partakes of the science of physics. How could an *infant* do it?

Another infant, of about the same age, suddenly picks up a violin, one of the most difficult of all musical instruments because it requires years of practice to gain the degree of dexterity necessary to play this unique instrument. This infant plays the violin exquisitely.

Still another infant, after watching his father play chess *twice*, announces that he is capable of playing and defeating his father at chess. He not only *does* so, but when taken to a chess club, swiftly defeats almost every chess player present.

I have made reference, of course, to Frederic Chopin, Wolfgang Amadeus Mozart and the Cuban chess-master (eventually chess-champion of the world) Jose Capablanca.

There are hundreds upon hundreds of other examples in art, in science, in virtually every field of endeavor, where children of an extremely tender age have exhibited not just extraordinary intelligence but a degree of sophistication that could only have been attained in a *previous* existence.

If you feel that all this is circumstantial evidence rather than direct evidence, let's consider some cases of remembered previous lives. You must have read at least one of the authenticated accounts of children who have (after recovery from a severe illness) lost all memory of their present life but had total recall of a previous life.

It is difficult not to sympathize with the shock and fright of a young child who wakes up in a strange bed, in a strange house and strange people who insist they are the parents.

We can also sympathize with the parents who cannot understand the vehement denial by the child as to their parenthood. They can only assume that the child is suffering from hallucination due to the severity of the illness.

Its understandable that faced with such a situation it would be difficult for a child to remain calm and not become completely hysterical. Even a mature person, in excellent health, would find it difficult to remain calm.

However there have been many instances where the child did remain calm and managed to give a clearly detailed description of his or her life right up to the moment before she fell asleep; the night before she awoke in the strange bed.

In each of the instances where the parents took the trouble to verify the child's story, it was found to be true and accurate in every detail. They would find, in the city described by the child, that there had been a boy or girl by that name. That the description of her parents, the house she lived in, the school she or he had attended, was fully accurate.

The child was the child of that other period of time and place, perhaps fifty, sixty or a hundred years ago.

In many instances that memory would fade away and be replaced by the present memory and the child's life would be resumed as though nothing unusual had happened. In other, more tragic instances, the present memory did not return and the child would be forced to take on a life that was, in all respects, completely alien and unhappy.

Older people have also suddenly and inexplicably—sometimes through shock or severe illness—reverted to the memory of a previous lifetime. In some cases their futile and pathetic efforts to return to their 'home and family' have caused considerable difficulty with the authorities.

Suppose, for a moment, that you suddenly felt faint or nauseous during a shopping trip and decided that you'd better go home and lie down. Only when you arrived home you discovered that complete strangers had taken possession of your home. You would be shocked and when you had recovered from the shock, called the police.

The police, on arrival, would easily verify the fact that the people living in your house had every right to be there. When you attempted to appeal to the neighbors you would discover that they were all strangers who had no knowledge of you at all. If you had no identification, you would, most likely (considering your state of mind at this time) be confined for mental observation and most likely be diagnosed as completely disoriented and mentally unbalanced.

In addition to the cases we have just mentioned, there are also the cases of people who have recalled, under hypnosis, many previous lives in astonishing detail. They have even spoken in the dialects of languages they have no knowledge of.

We also have, most recently, documented cases of people who have 'died' and, upon being revived, have been able to recount in vivid detail, exactly what happened to them from the moment they 'died' until they were brought back.

In reading these accounts we have to be struck by the amazing similarity to the description of the after-death experiences described in the Tibetan Book Of The Dead.

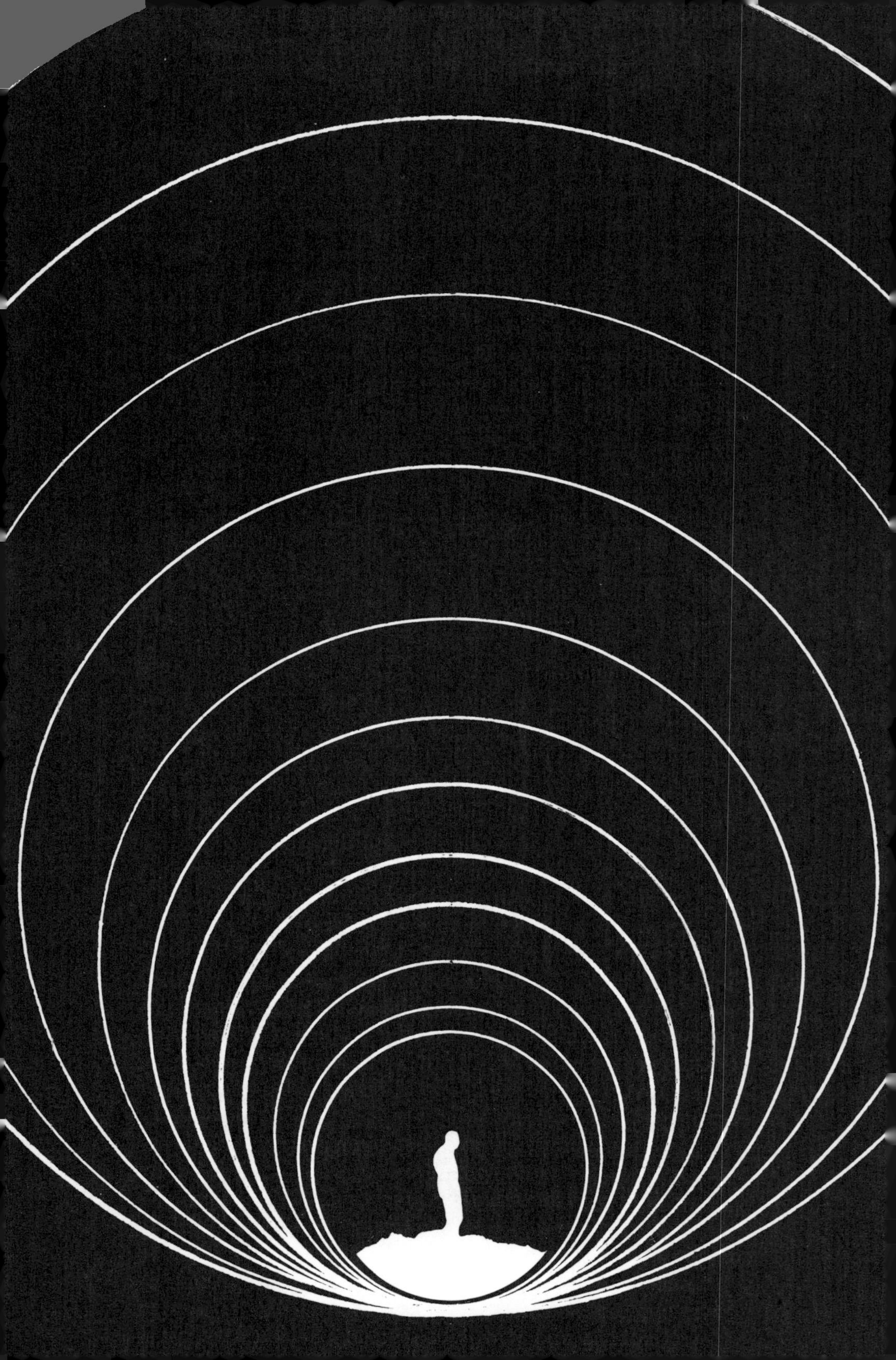

*Come, lovely and soothing death,
undulate around the world, serenely
arriving, arriving in the day, in the
night, to all, to each, sooner or
later, delicate death.*
    WHITMAN

The 'out-of-body' experience that these people were able to recall—even though they were handicapped by the *dimensional blindness* we discussed earlier—gave a clear and understandable account of what happens in those moments when they are literally at death's door. For periods of time which range from a few moments to as much as twenty and thirty minutes, there was a serious question as to whether they will die or continue to live.

All of the accounts that have been made public stress two important aspects of this 'death'. The first is that they are a complete entity, regardless of the condition of their human body—for example after a *violent* accident. They are *aware* of everything that is happening—can see everything clearly—can see exactly what is being done to bring them back to life.

The most remarkable thing is that *all* of them describe the scene—whether it's in a hospital room—at home, on the street where the accident took place—wherever it is—it's described from an *impossible* viewpoint (from a three-dimensional standpoint). They are describing what they see from *above*, rather than on the same level.

In other words, they were in a world with *more* dimensions than our visible world.

The most significant item in their accounts—to me at least—was the mention of the *tunnel of blackness*. Each of them, at the moment of approaching death, was thrust into, or rushed through, a tube—a tunnel—a channel—or a corridor of blackness towards a light at the other end.

I can recall at least two occasions—while under ether or gas (and I realize now that I was probably dying of an overdose) when I found myself racing down a long black corridor towards a light at the other end. I was extremely happy, for some reason and then became extremely unhappy when I was rudely yanked back and became conscious again.

It all happened so swiftly that I forgot about it until I began to read about the many 'out-of-body' accounts of the people who had 'died' and then come back to life.

I only regret that I didn't reach the point where the 'being of light' appeared. This is one of the most assuring aspects of these many accounts.

In each instance, the people who have undergone these 'other world' experiences, have clearly described the warmth and genuine concern expressed by this 'being of light'. In every instance, after the initial shock of finding themselves in this odd environment, the people involved have stated that they were relaxed, comfortable and had no fear at all.

There is another branch of 'out of body' experience that startled me even more than those of people who had apparently (or clinically) 'died'—this concerned people who suddenly had an out-of-body experience without any of the trauma connected with violent injury of 'death' from 'natural' causes.

My first encounter was with a doctor—a friend of long standing—who had never discussed anything of a 'psychical' nature with me nor I with him because I sensed extreme resistance on his part to the notion of anything 'unnatural'.

I was quite surprised, one evening, when he suggested that we take a walk to a nearby delicatessen—ostensibly to get a six-pack of beer. It was a fair distance away—possibly a half mile—and even though it was a pleasant evening, it was a bit of a hike for him.

I was about to ask him if he would like me to drive him there and then thought better of it. He obviously wanted to talk rather than walk—and he wanted to talk away from the house and out of possible 'eavesdropping' by his wife.

I wondered if I was about to hear some confession of wrongdoing or possibly a marital problem and braced myself for a role of intermediary which happened quite often in my relationships with friends and acquaintances.

Neither of us spoke for at least five minutes during our leisurely walk. He spent most of the time fussing with his pipe—cleaning it—scraping it—tapping it and blowing noisily through the stem to clear away particles of tobacco.

I began to wonder if I'd been mistaken. Perhaps he really did want to buy a six-pack and really did want to take a walk. I relaxed and enjoyed the pleasant night air and the aroma of grass that has been cut late in the afternoon.

"Do you know anything about out-of-body experiences?"

The question dumbfounded me. He was the last person in the world I would expect that kind of a question from.

"A little," I said cautiously. "Why?"

He didn't answer me immediately, just kept walking, fooling with the pipe, and clearing his throat occasionally.

"Have you ever experienced it?" He asked, finally and the tone of his voice was completely casual, as though it was just a subject for conversational purposes but I began to suspect that there was more to it than that.

"I had two experiences that could be called OOBE's."

"Really?" He sounded a little relieved and I got the impression that he had been apprehensive about my reply. Now I was certain that there was a serious reason behind his invitation to 'take a walk to the deli' and waited more patiently for him to open up and begin talking.

"They're referred to as OOBE's?" He sounded as though he were talking to himself—thinking aloud rather than talking to me. "That would indicate that they're a fairly common experience?"

"Well—I think wide-spread, rather than common."
"I see." He nodded several times and then added, "and you—actually—have had two—OOBE's."
"Yes."
"You think they were real experiences or just—well illusions—I hate to use the word hallucinations because it sounds almost rude. You know?"
"I understand. They were real—not imagined—if that's what you're trying to say."
"That's what I mean. I just couldn't think of the word. Imagined. Exactly. You don't think you imagined them?"
"No. I think I did—at first—until I began to discover there were other people who had the same experience."
"Ah!" He seemed pleased now. "You mean that you did think it was imaginary until you read that other people had similar experiences and then you decided it was real."
"No. There was more to it than just that." I realized that I was becoming defensive and paused to swing my thinking around put the shoe on the other foot. "Why don't you tell me about *your* OOBE's, Ralph?"

He didn't say anything for a moment or two and then he smiled and shook his head slowly.

"You're quick," he said. "I'll give you that."
"Not quick, Ralph—just a little intuitive."
"So you think that OOBE's are real and not imagined."
"Yes."

He then began to tell me of a series of disturbing incidents. His first experience was so swift and fleeting that he passed it off as a dream.

"I was lying awake in bed one night," he said slowly as though remembering it and trying to describe it exactly the way it happened without embellishment. "There was a full moon and the curtain wasn't fully closed so a shaft of moonlight seemed to pierce the darkness and fall on the foot of the bed. I was lying there watching the dust motes rising lazily and the next thing I knew I was *floating up*, just like the dust motes. I remember putting up my hand so that I wouldn't bump into the ceiling and I was shocked when my hand went right through the ceiling."

He stopped and I realized that he was staring straight ahead and I was certain that he was re-living that odd experience and so I waited for a few moments. Finally I couldn't control my impatience. I coughed and said,

"Ralph?" He didn't answer and I tapped his arm.
"What? Oh—sorry—I was lost in thought."
"What happened after your hand went through the ceiling? Did you keep on going up?"
"Oh no. I was so shocked—I sort of froze up—and the next thing I knew I was sitting up, in bed, shaking all over. I felt ice cold even though it was a hot June night. I began to review what I'd eaten for supper that could cause such a nightmare and then—after a few moments I went to sleep."
"Tell me about the others."
"How do you know there were others?"
"Come on, Ralph. If that was the only experience you would have forgotten about it."
"What makes you so smart? You must be thirty?"
"Thirty-one. I'm not smart—just well read."
"Umm. Well, you're right. There were others. Listen. I hope what I'm telling you is—well—strictly between us. I don't want anybody—not even—well—you know what I mean. This is confidential—understand."

"You know better, Ralph. There's no need to say that."

"You're right. I shouldn't have said that. It's just that I've been carrying this thing around for so long—scared to death that Martha would find out—and you know how excitable she is. Ah—it was stupid of me."

"Just tell me about the other experiences, Ralph."

"Well—about a month later—I think it was towards the end of July—I was alone—Martha had gone to some club meeting and I thought I'd take a nap on the sofa. Well actually—I was watching TV and I decided to lie down on the sofa and watch it—maybe I guessed I'd fall asleep—I don't know. Anyway I was lying on my side and my hand was hanging over the edge of the sofa—you know—I was resting my head on the pillow and my arm was under the pillow so my hand was hanging out and I wondered if it would fall asleep and I wanted to move it but I was just too comfortable.

"Anyway—I think I'd fallen asleep—and I either dreamt or imagined that somebody took hold of my hand—very gently—and I thought it was Martha and she wanted me to get up and go to bed. So I nodded and started to get up and I had the oddest sensation. I don't know how to say it."

He paused, and I could see that he was trying to find a way to describe the sensation and I waited patiently for him to continue. I found it difficult to resist helping him—I *knew* what he was trying to say but it would have been *wrong* for me to tell him *how* to say it—he had to do that himself. That was the only way he could come to grips with it.

"The only way I can describe it," he said finally, "it's like—have you ever dived down to the bottom of a swimming pool—stayed on the bottom for awhile and then, at the last minute, pushed up and moved to the top? Do you remember the sudden relief of being up—in the air—breathing again?

Well that's what it was like. I sort of *slid out of myself* and was suddenly relieved and breathing easier than I had in my life before and I wondered why I felt so good. I opened my eyes, expecting to see Martha—but there was nobody there—and I realized that I was passing right through the roof of the house out into the night! I was shocked and terribly frightened. I yanked my hand away from whatever was holding it and there was a thump! And there I was on the couch—sweating and my heart pumping madly.

"I was really frightened. I sat up and tried to figure out what was wrong with me. It was obvious that I was having some kind of a recurring nightmare. I remembered the other dream about putting my hand through the ceiling and wondered how many other dreams I'd had that I didn't remember—or didn't want to remember."

"So what was your diagnosis, Ralph?"

"Indigestion. Only for the life of me I couldn't remember eating anything different. But it had to be indigestion. I sincerely hoped at the time that that's what it was."

"But you had more OOBE's?"

"Oh, yes. My God, yes. Worse than ever."

"Worse how?"

"I began to have them more frequently. It would happen almost anytime I'd relax—really relax—it started to happen while I was driving and that scared the hell out of me. I haven't driven a car since. I can't. I don't dare take the chance. I tell you—I'm almost at the end of my rope. I can't tell anyone—I mean how could I? They'd assume that I was losing my mind. I have a very good practice—I can't afford to lose that. I just don't know what the hell's happening to me."

"Ralph, I'm going to say something that may sound outrageous in light of what you're going through but I have to say it. I would give my right arm to be in your place. I mean that, Ralph."

"That's not outrageous—that's insane!"

"I'm quite serious, Ralph. Do you know how long I've been trying to do exactly what you do—so easily?"

"You don't know what you're talking about!" he was really angry. "There's nothing pleasurable about what's been happening to me. It's horrible!"

"I know exactly what's been happening to you and it's not horrible at all—it's a fabulous gift."

"What do you mean—you know exactly what's been happening—you just said you've never been able to—"

"I know because you're not the first person this has ever happened to, Ralph. It's been happening to people for thousands of years."

"Of course it has—and it's called insanity."

"It is not insanity—it's reality. It's something you were born to do—we all were. You're just more fortunate than most people because you can do it naturally."

"Do what? What am I doing?"

Then I began to tell him, exactly what I've just told you that there is a dimension beyond this Earth's dimension. I showed him the experiments with two-dimensional beings and he began to understand the reason for his ability to move through solid objects as easily as sunlight pierces the window.

I also explained to him that he had complete *control* over his actions. He merely had to 'will' himself to return to his physical body and it was accomplished in nanoseconds. That further he *now* had a way to discover the truth about 'death' before he actually 'died' and this should be a great comfort.

I told him about the people who had 'died' had a vivid experience in the 'other' dimension and then reunited with their physical body and were 'changed' from that moment on. They were calmer—more empathetic—and many of them developed extraordinary insight and capabilities.

In essence they were 'altered' by their experience just as he would be, once he understood the nature of the 'gift'.

I've seen Ralph many times since that night. He's really a changed man—a much happier man—with an extraordinary calmness which astonishes people.

* * *

The case histories you are about to read have been collected from many different sources. Some are from personal encounters; some are from newspaper accounts; others were supplied by people who knew of my interest.

The gymnasium, at the high school I attended, had several 'climbing ropes' which, when used correctly were perfectly safe. Daredevils, like Robert B., rarely used them correctly and, on more than one occasion, narrowly escaped serious injury. I remember a particular incident when Bob decided to imitate a stunt employed by an aerialist we had both seen at the circus over the weekend. The aerialist had descended from his trapeze, via the rope head-first and Bob was determined to try it as soon as the gym teacher left the area. I begged him not to do it because it seemed to me that you had to have considerable training to do a stunt like that.

He insisted that he was not going to 'chicken out' just because *I* was afraid to do it. I debated whether I should warn the gym teacher but the 'code' against snitching prevented that. I just had to watch helplessly while Bob climbed the rope which was at least thirty feet above the gym floor.

When he reached the top, he swung around, twined his legs around the rope, stretched out and began his descent. He started down, slowly at first, and then—something happened. I don't know whether the rope burnt his hand or whether he picked up a rope splinter, but he suddenly came down with a

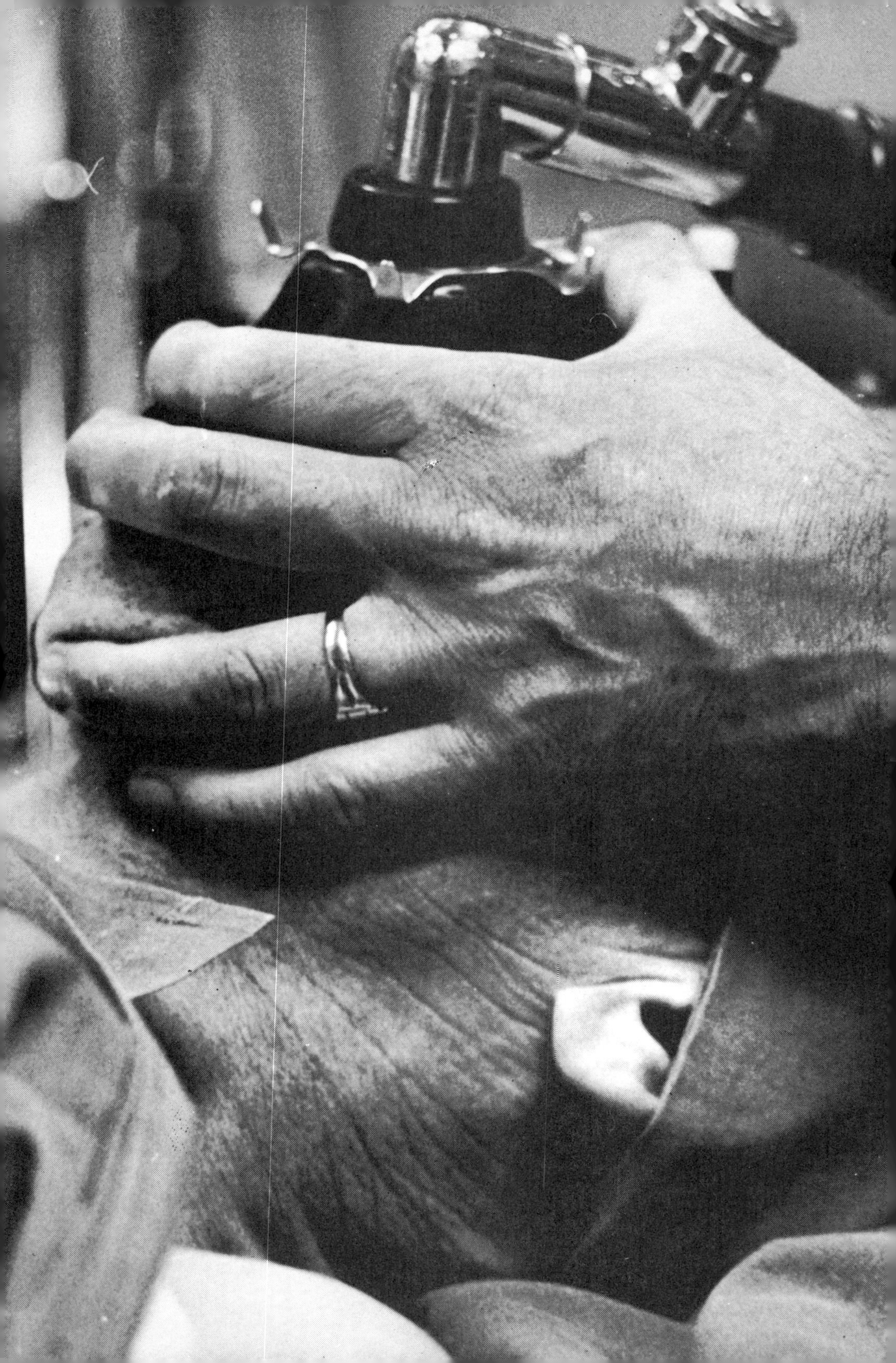

*Where there
is no vision,
the people perish.*
　　　　PROVERBS XXIX

terrible *thump*! as his head struck the hardwood floor and I screamed for the gym teacher because the blood was all over. I remember I was crying—and they let me go in the ambulance with him but then, when we got to the hospital they sent me home and I could tell by the way everybody acted that Bob had died in the ambulance.

I felt a terrible sense of guilt. It was my fault because I didn't warn the gym teacher and the worse part was that everyone was so decent to me.

Then, late that night, about ten o'clock, Bob's parents called my folks and told them that it was a miracle but Bob was alive and the doctor said he was going to be all right. I wasn't asleep and I heard my father talking on the phone so I came out of my bedroom and went to the head of the stairs. I can't describe the enormous sense of sheer relief when my father told me that Bob was alive. It was like a reprieve.

When I went to see Bob in the hospital I asked him what he'd thought when he realized that he was going to hit the floor. I have never forgotten what he said to me or the amazingly calm way he talked.

"I knew what was going to happen as soon as I started down," he said slowly and he was looking past me as though he was seeing it all over again. "I knew I was going to hit the floor—and I knew I was going to die when I did."

"You knew? Weren't you scared?"

"At first—just for a second—my stomach froze and I wanted to scream—but before I could open my mouth—wham! It was just like an explosion—only there was no pain! I was suddenly floating—it felt like I was floating in warm water—and I felt so good I was surprised—really surprised because I don't ever remember feeling that good before." He was smiling quietly and his face looked different. He didn't seem like the same person.

85

"Did you think you were dead?"

"I didn't think it," he said calmly and looked straight at me, "I knew I was dead."

"But—you couldn't have been—you're here!"

"No." He shook his head and smiled that odd smile. "I was dead but they didn't want me to stay, so they sent me back."

"What do you mean—'they'—who? The doctors?"

"I don't know who they were. I remember there was a long, black tunnel and I could see a light at the other end, so I started towards it—not walking—sort of floating—only I didn't move my hands or feet—I just thought that I wanted to go to the end of the tunnel—to the light—and I just moved.

"What kind of a light?"

"I don't know."

"Didn't you see what it was when you got there?"

"No," he said slowly and thoughtfully, "because I never reached it. They stopped me before I reached the end.

"Who stopped you?"

"I don't know. I never saw them. I could just feel them turning me, very gently, and saying that I had to go back. I didn't want to go back."

"You mean—you *wanted* to be dead?" I was astonished. He had always been the most 'alive' person I'd ever known.

"Yes." he said calmly and smiled that odd smile again and I had the most uneasy feeling that he wasn't the same Bob that I had known for so long.

"Why didn't you want to come back to life? Don't you enjoy being alive?"

"Yes, but you have to understand what it was like. It was being *more* alive than—really being alive."

"That's crazy talk!" I was frightened now because I began to think that he wasn't 'right' in his head. The fall must have damaged his brain and that's what made him talk like that.

"No it's not." he said softly. "Someday you'll find out and then you'll understand."

"Okay, Bob. Let's talk about something else."

We changed the subject and I never spoke about it again and neither did he. But I never forgot it.

Maybe, underneath my anger and fright, I realized that he'd been telling the truth. All I know is that I started reading everything I could find about 'death'.

I soon discovered that there was considerable controversy with regard to the 'nature' of death and that surprised me because I thought that all the great thinkers in the past were quite settled on the subject. They were not—nor are they today.

I also discovered two remarkable works—the Egyptian Book of the Dead and the Tibetian Book of the Dead. Both dealt with the effect upon Man after dying, when Man enters a different world.

The Egyptian Book of the Dead seemed rather fanciful to me—perhaps because it had become so ritualistic that the original meaning and truth was obscured. But the Tibetian Book of the Dead told me a lot of things that reminded me of what Bob had said about his 'death' and Bob had never, as far as I know, read—or knew anything about Tibet or their Book of the Dead.

The Tibetans believed that it was important to inform the dying that they were dying because if they didn't, the dead person wouldn't realize what had happened to him. He would be confused, because he would be able to see and hear everything at his funeral and instead of entering into his 'other' life would stay here on this plane and cause suffering and hardship to his loved ones—and other people in the community. He would become a troublesome 'ghost'.

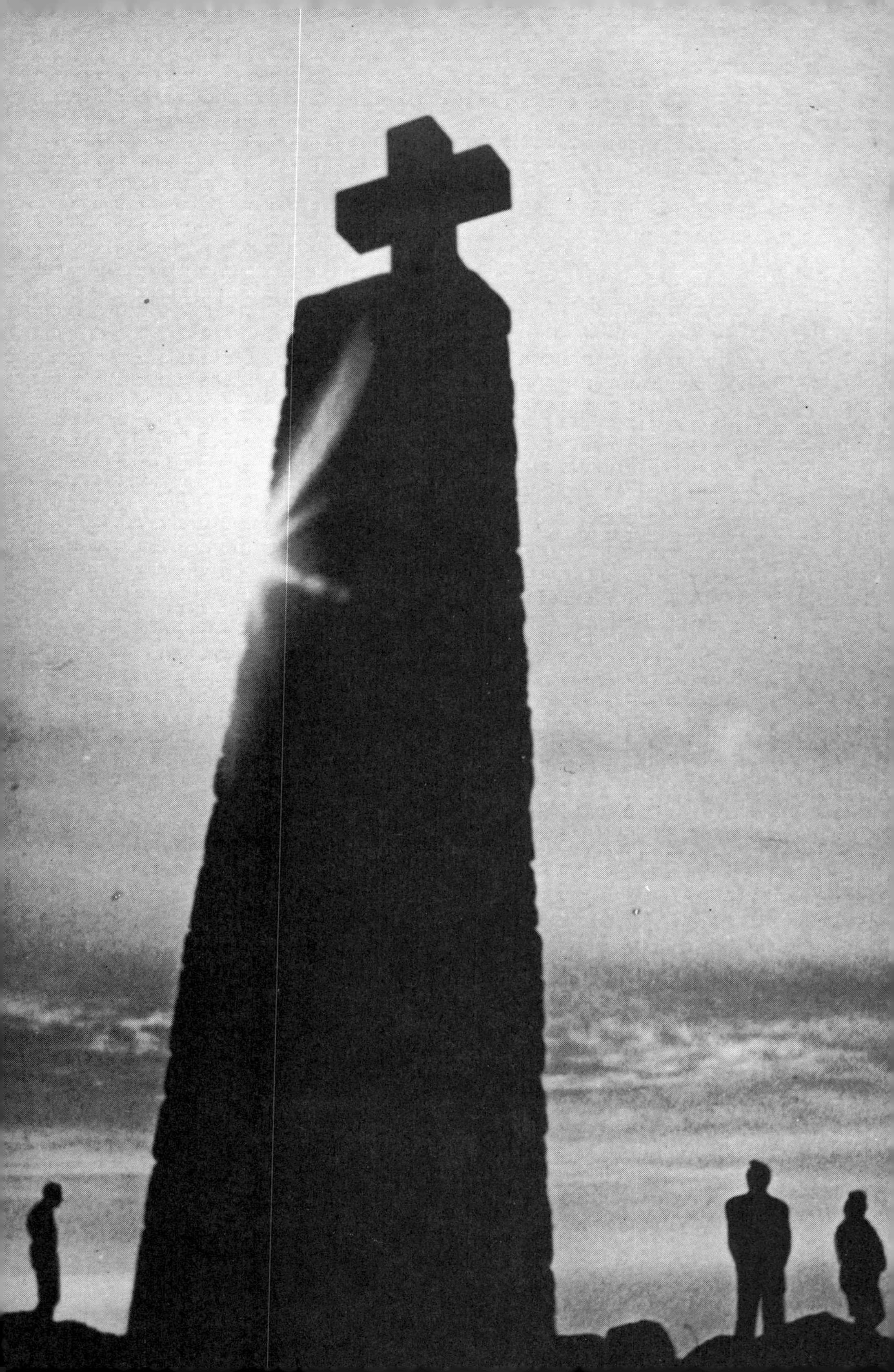

If we submit everything to reason, our religion will have nothing in it mysterious or supernatural. If we violate the principles of reason then our religion will be absurd and ridiculous.
　　　　　　　　　　PASCAL

So the wise men—the men who had 'experienced' death and returned—created the Book of the Dead which explained exactly what happened to a person after they died. It told of the transition from a physical body to a non-physical entity and the surprise that 'consciousness' still existed. The entity would hear many alarming noises and would find himself in some kind of a swirling mist of light. He would feel as though he had a new body—a perfect body and he would discover that his mind seemed to be very clear and he could 'see' many things such as his entire life—coolly and objectively. He would, in effect, be able to 'judge' himself dispassionately.

With the training that he received from the wise men—and the Book of the Dead—he would know that it was 'wrong' for him to move into the 'other' life.

The more I read—the more accounts I found—the closer I came to the realization that all of these incidents—even when they were thousands of years apart—were strikingly similar. So much so that it became plain to me that 'death' is *not*—as Shakespeare said—"*the undiscovered country from whose bourn no traveler returns...*"

Many travelers have returned—just as Bob did.

A friend, Larry W., told this account of his 'death'.

"We were playing 'one night stands'—doing shows each night in towns that were sometimes two or three hundred miles apart. I did most of the driving and it was difficult to get enough sleep what with making all the arrangements—setting the stage—seeing to the props—rounding up the actors in time for the show—and then, after acting in the show myself, starting all over to pack everything up and start driving to the next town. It was hard to do on two or three hours sleep.

I remember, we'd just arrived, about two o'clock in the afternoon, at this one town and the first thing I did, after unpacking everything, was to fall into bed.

I hadn't been asleep more than a half hour when they woke me up and said the producer was on the phone calling long distance and it was some kind of an emergency.

I was so tired I could hardly see, but I threw on some clothes and stumbled downstairs to the desk phone (we didn't have them in the rooms at this place) and listened to the producer tell me that our engagement had been cancelled and I had to set up the stage in the theatre in another town about sixty miles away.

I told him that I was dead on my feet and just couldn't do it. He screamed about a 'forfeit bond' of two thousand dollars and acted like a madman on the phone. So I finally said that I'd go—although it would probably be the death of me if I did. That wasn't just idle talk—I had a premonition that something was going to happen.

He did too, because I found out later that he'd called back after I left to try to stop me from going. But it was too late. I'd roared away in the truck and was on my way to an appointment with death.

I remember that I was driving too fast but kept telling myself that (1) by driving that fast I wouldn't *dare* to fall asleep at the wheel and (2) driving that fast would get me there quicker and I'd have more time to sleep.

The end came on a sharp, almost hairpin turn that I must have hit at about eighty-five miles an hour. I never made it. I was sound asleep and I remember the sound of metal ripping, immediately followed by an explosion of some kind and I thought—this is it. This is really it.

I fully expected to feel terrible pain and tried to brace myself against the shock and the ripping and tearing that would follow the impact—but nothing happened!

I opened my eyes cautiously and was astonished to find that I was in some kind of a thick fog. It was luminous, as though there were headlights just beyond it and I thought they were probably police cars or maybe the ambulance.

Then suddenly the fog lifted and I could see everything quite clearly. I was looking down, from about a hundred feet in the air, at the highway below me and what was left of the company's truck. It had crashed through a stone abutment on the far side of the curve and was hanging, half over the conduit that allowed a small stream to pass under the highway. Scenery and baggage was strewn over the highway and some of it was in the stream.

I was surprised that it wasn't burning because of the explosion that I'd heard. I was also surprised at how calm I was. I was looking at it as though it had nothing to do with me.

Everything was so quiet I thought for a moment that I just couldn't *hear* anything and then—way off—I heard a train whistling a crossing—and I realized that the crash must have scared every bird in the area.

Then I heard a car coming and I watched it slow down and stop and two men jumped out and ran to the truck.

"There's nobody here!" One of them yelled and the other one said, "Look around—he might have been thrown clear."

So I started to look around too—and then I saw this body—half hidden in the cattails on the side of the bank.

"There he is!" One of them yelled and pointed. They climbed down the abutment and I drifted down to take a look, too. It wasn't a pretty sight. It looked a bloody mess and I could see the bone sticking out of the thigh—right through the pants.

"Jesus!" One of the men said and the other one started to get sick and I wondered why they were so upset because I wasn't—and it was me down there.

91

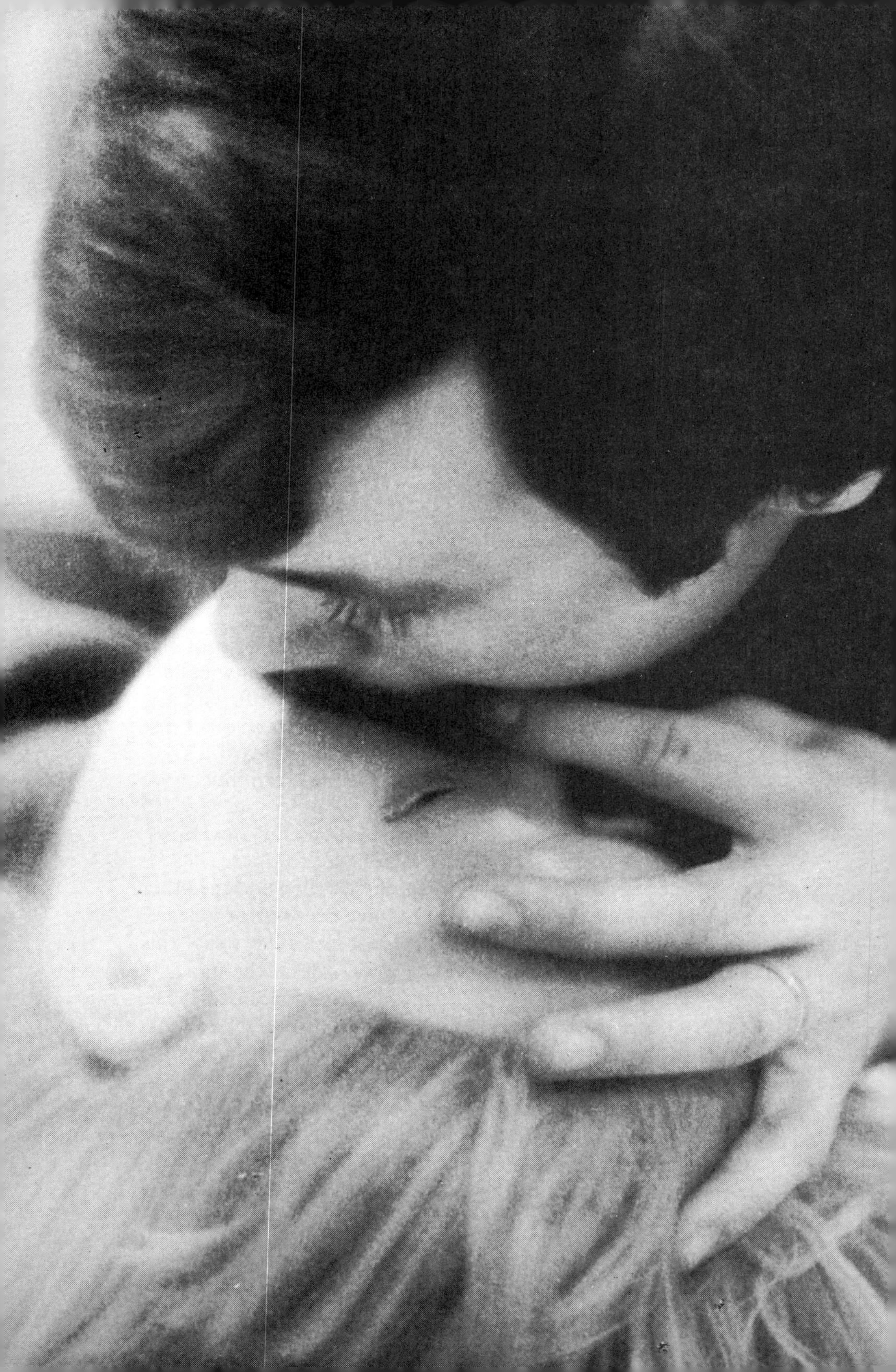

*Life is the one universal soul
which by virtue of the enlivening
Breath and the informing
Word, all organized bodies have
in common, each after its kind.*
      COLERIDGE

I lost interest then, and drifted back up and the mist closed in again and got darker and I thought, *well—here we go and I wonder what's going to happen?*

Then—suddenly—I was in some kind of a tunnel—I remember that it was very narrow—and that I was moving through it at a pretty good clip. It didn't worry me because I could see a light at the end and figured that's where I was going.

Then a strange thing happened. I slowed down and a voice spoke to me—at least I think so—because I heard someone say—inside my head—which is the only way I can describe it—

"Do you really want to?"

Then everything stopped and I sort of hung there—and then slowly the darkness went away and I was looking down—from the ceiling—at the doctors and nurses running back and forth—doing all kinds of things.

And I wondered why they were bothering because it must have been obvious that I was dead. I remember this one doctor who was sweating—his green blouse was soaked and his face mask was soggy and he was cursing steadily but without any anger. It was very strange.

I remember looking at my face and it didn't look like me at all but I knew that it was me—or part of me. I'd never seen my face so white. It was like white marble—almost as white as the bandages that swathed the top of my head.

I was surprised at all the blood. It was everywhere. There were bloody bandages and pads and the doctors were bloody up to their elbows.

Then something nudged me gently.

"You have to go back now." It was that same voice in my head and I didn't want to go back into that bloody body. That was the last thing I wanted to do. I wanted to go back to the tunnel and the light and find out what was on the other side. But I kept feeling this gentle nudging.

The last thing I remember is someone saying,
"He's going to make it."
And the next thing I knew I was awake in this bed and my producer was sitting there with his head in his hands and I said,
"Did we forfeit the bond?"

There was more to the story—but that's the part that's important. Except for the fact that Larry was *different* after that. Just like Bob was different.

I lost touch with Larry, shortly after he told me about his experience with 'death'. Some friends told me that he was teaching school some place in the South and was very happy.

There was a case of a woman who 'died' while giving birth to a baby because of unforeseen complications. She described a sensation of a tiny explosion—almost like a ping! And the next thing she knew she was looking down at her body on the operating table and there was obviously something wrong because they were wheeling in this strange equipment and everybody seemed to be under some kind of a strain.

"I knew that I was dying and that didn't seem to matter. I wondered if they would be able to save the baby but I wasn't very concerned about it. Nothing seemed to be important.
It didn't seem to be happening to me—but to that person on the table. Even though I knew it *was* me I didn't really care. I was interested in everything that was going on—it was like a movie—because it didn't seem real—and yet it was very real. That sounds contradictory but it's the only way I can explain the way I felt about it.
Then there was another ping! And everything was blooted out. I was all alone in some kind of a blackish void only there was light around the edges. I wondered what I was supposed to do. Would somebody come for me or was I supposed to figure it out myself?

I wasn't upset. On the contrary I never felt better. My body felt marvelous and I wasn't pregnant—it was almost as though I was a young girl again.

I remember a sensation of motion, only I wasn't doing anything. The mist was getting blacker and blacker and I thought—is it going to be black all the time?

But I wasn't frightened—just curious.

Then, suddenly I was in this big place. It was lighted but very softly and there was a sort of canyon and on the other side there were people—a lot of people and they just looked at me with no expression and I thought I recognized one or two of them but I wasn't sure.

I wanted to get closer to the people but I couldn't figure out how to get across the canyon. It sounds silly but the canyon seemed to be some kind of a barrier even though a barrier is supposed to be something that sticks up rather than a huge, empty gash in the earth.

Then the people on the other side turned away and I thought—they've given up. Why are they giving up?

I realized that I was being turned around even though I couldn't feel anyone touching me—somebody was turning me—very gently but firmly and I didn't want to go.

Then I felt myself moving away and a terrible sadness came over me because I knew I had to go back and I didn't want to go back. Someone said,

"It's all right—you can come back here someday."

And I felt a little better because I realized that it was the truth. I would be back again someday. And after that it was all right again and I didn't mind going back.

I don't remember anything after that—just that I was in bed and the doctor was holding my wrist and smiling and I felt all washed out and terribly tired.

* * *

It seems that every time I find a particular kind of an experience I run across a half-dozen more. A lot of women apparently 'die' during childbirth and return. Most of them tell very similar stories. Some of the details may vary but the overall message is plainly similar.

What about out-of-body experiences where 'death' didn't play a direct part? There have been many cases recorded where people have been 'visited' by people who have died. In some cases the 'live' people have visited the 'dead'.

These are not 'dream' experiences but 'real' events.

Lillian B. Told me the following story:

"I had just come from visiting my sister, who was terminally ill (cancer) and I was sitting downstairs in the living room thinking of how wasted she'd looked. She was so thin—just bones—and she'd been so beautiful both as a child and as a young woman—and it seemed so unfair because she knew what had happened to her.

I remember that I started to cry and was astonished to hear someone whisper, "Don't cry, Lillian. It's all right now. I'm just fine. Really I am."

I looked up in shock and my sister was standing there and she was beautiful and there was such a look of serenity on her face it took my breath away. She was just radiant. She nodded slowly at me as though she was satisfied and then she faded away and I knew that I was wide awake and not dreaming and that I had actually seen my sister.

I don't know why but I suddenly felt a tremendous sense of relief and thankfulness. I was actually happy.

The phone was ringing and as I got up from my chair to answer it I knew that it was my mother calling me.

"Oh, Lillian," my mother said in a choked voice, "She's gone." She was crying.

"I know, Mother. I just saw her."

"I don't understand. Did you hear what I said?"

"Yes, Mother—she was just here—and she looked just beautiful and contented and—it's really all right."

My mother never really believed me. She insisted that I had been dreaming but I *know* that I was awake and that I did see my sister and the reason she came to me was to comfort me. And she succeeded."

* * *

There have been literally thousands of recorded incidents like this over the years but they have been discounted as 'dreams' or 'imaginings' or 'wish fulfillment' until recent years with the considerable interest that has taken place in OOBE's (Out Of Body Experiences)

* * *

One of the most interesting aspects I've noted, in the many cases I've recorded over the years, is the number of times I've been told of *"seeing my whole life before me."*

It has intrigued me because, until recently, scientists have tended to discount the notion that—*as you die your whole life flashes before you.*

Professor Peter S. at the university gave me some insight into that aspect of dying. He'd suddenly been stricken with a heart attack in the middle of one of his classes (a year before I met him) and had been rushed to the hospital.

"When the pain hit me—and just before I became unconscious—I knew that it was the end. I was fully prepared for it because I'd been warned about the possibility of a really strong one—and this was it.

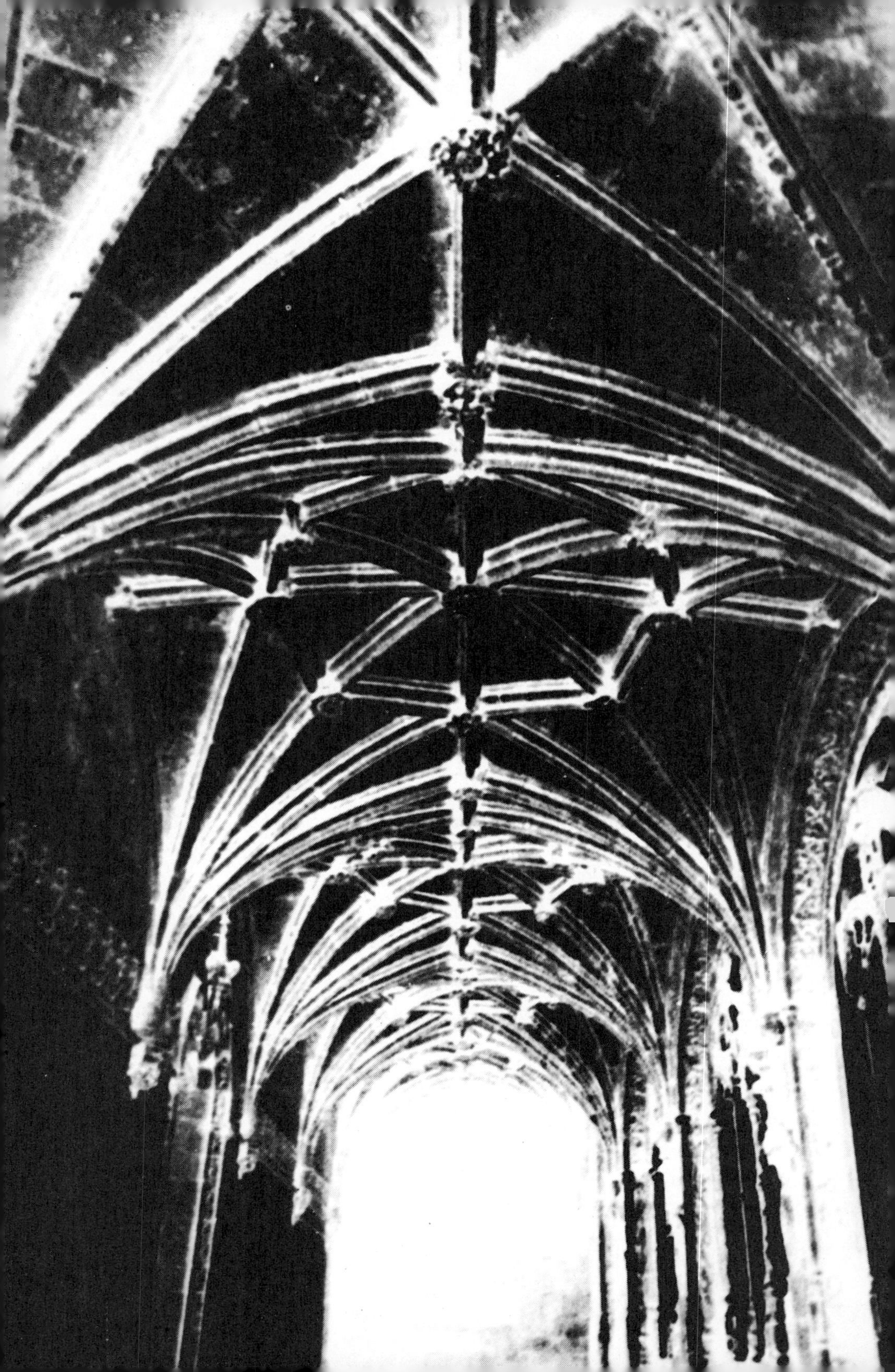

*The grave itself is
but a covered bridge
leading from light
to light through a
brief darkness.*
    LONGFELLOW

I had no regrets. My affairs were all in order. I was leaving no one behind me to mourn—except for the possibility that some of my students might have shed a tear. So I left this world with a sense of sheer relief and, I must confess, considerable curiosity about what would happen to me.

My first sensation was that I was moving, quite swiftly through some kind of a dark corridor—similar to the corridors here at the university—except that it was really black. I remember wondering what the rush was all about—because now I had all the time in the world. My second thought was—ho ho—there is something after death—and then I wondered if I was going to face the music for the life I'd lived.

Then I noticed a light, up ahead, in the darkness. I wondered if that would be the judge's chamber. Would I be permitted to retain counsel or would I be expected to defend myself? It may sound odd but that's exactly what went through my mind as I approached the light.

I was surprised when I reached it—only that's not quite right—I didn't reach it—it reached *me*. I think the truth is that I stayed put—even though I thought I was moving—and the light came to me. Does that make any sense? Well, whether it does or not—the light came.

That's exactly what it was—a light—a pervasive kind of light that seemed to flow into everything and you were only conscious of the light and—something else that's almost impossible to describe. How can I say it? There was a warmth and loving regard that seemed to flow from that light—but that's such a weak way of describing it—you can't imagine the comfort that feeling gave me.

Then the most amazing thing happened. I 'saw' this little boy. He was playing at the dge of a pond and my first thought was—"*what's a little boy like that doing all by himself—he could fall in and drown—where the devil are his parents?*

99

And then I realized that I was that little boy! Then everything seemed to speed up—but not at all uncomfortably—but my life moved very rapidly along and I watched myself grow to manhood and was fully aware of a series of 'decisional highlights' that I had witnessed. It was each of the points in my life where I had to make a decision with regard to moral or ethical conduct and I regret to say that in most cases I made the wrong decision. There were, however, mitigating circumstances in many cases. My intentions were 'good' but my actions were stupid.

It was an extraordinary 'lesson' and I had a feeling that the warm being of the light—whoever it was—had given me a rare opportunity to make my own judgment as to the net worth of my life.

"Well," I asked impatiently, "did you give yourself a passing grade, at least?"

"No," he said with a sad smile, "I did not. I gave myself an 'F' and yet," his face lighted up, "I knew that I would be given another chance to do better."

"Are you doing better?"

"Yes, but that isn't what I meant. I meant in my next life."

"Did the 'light' tell you that?"

"No—even though I felt that was true. No, I found that other 'truth' by myself. You see, once I realized that it was possible to have an out-of-body experience, I began to investigate ways of producing those OOBE's without having to arrive at death's door."

"Did you find out how to do it?"

"Oh yes. That was the simplest part. You see, I had a head start because I had already realized that the key to it was in the partially unconscious state we assume just before waking or just before sleeping, each day of our lives. That—and a little auto-hypnosis—did the trick."

"What was the difficult part?"

"Concentrating. Keeping my mind firmly fixed on what I wanted to do, once I'd arrived at the disembodied condition that I was striving for."

"I don't understand why that should be difficult."

"It's a little hard to explain to—"

"Someone who's never been there," I concluded for him. "Just explain it any way you like—I'll try to keep up."

"All right. Take the matter of penetrating this plane of existence. That, in itself, is extremely difficult.

"Why should that be so difficult? After all *this is* where you belong. So why should you have to penetrate it at all. Why can't you just be here?"

"Because the fact is I don't belong here—neither do you—nobody really *belongs* here at all—we're just temporary visitors—transients. Do you understand?"

"You mean that it was more natural for you to be there than here—is that it?"

"That is precisely it. Here is just a part of there. A relatively unimportant part, I might add. It's a necessary part but not an important part if you follow me."

"I think you lost me, Professor. Everything that I've read points to the fact that we have to live successive lives in this plane of existence."

"For what purpose?"

"To learn to live 'perfect' lives I guess."

"Then what?"

"Well—when we achieve *that* I guess we move to the next plane above this one—right?"

"Exactly—and that's why I'm doing—reaching up and into the 'other' planes of existence to learn more about them."

"But aren't you supposed to be learning how to be 'good' in each lifetime? Doesn't this sort of defeat the whole purpose?"

"Ah—but you see, my boy, once you have been 'there' and returned you cannot be anything but 'good' whether you want to or not."

* * *

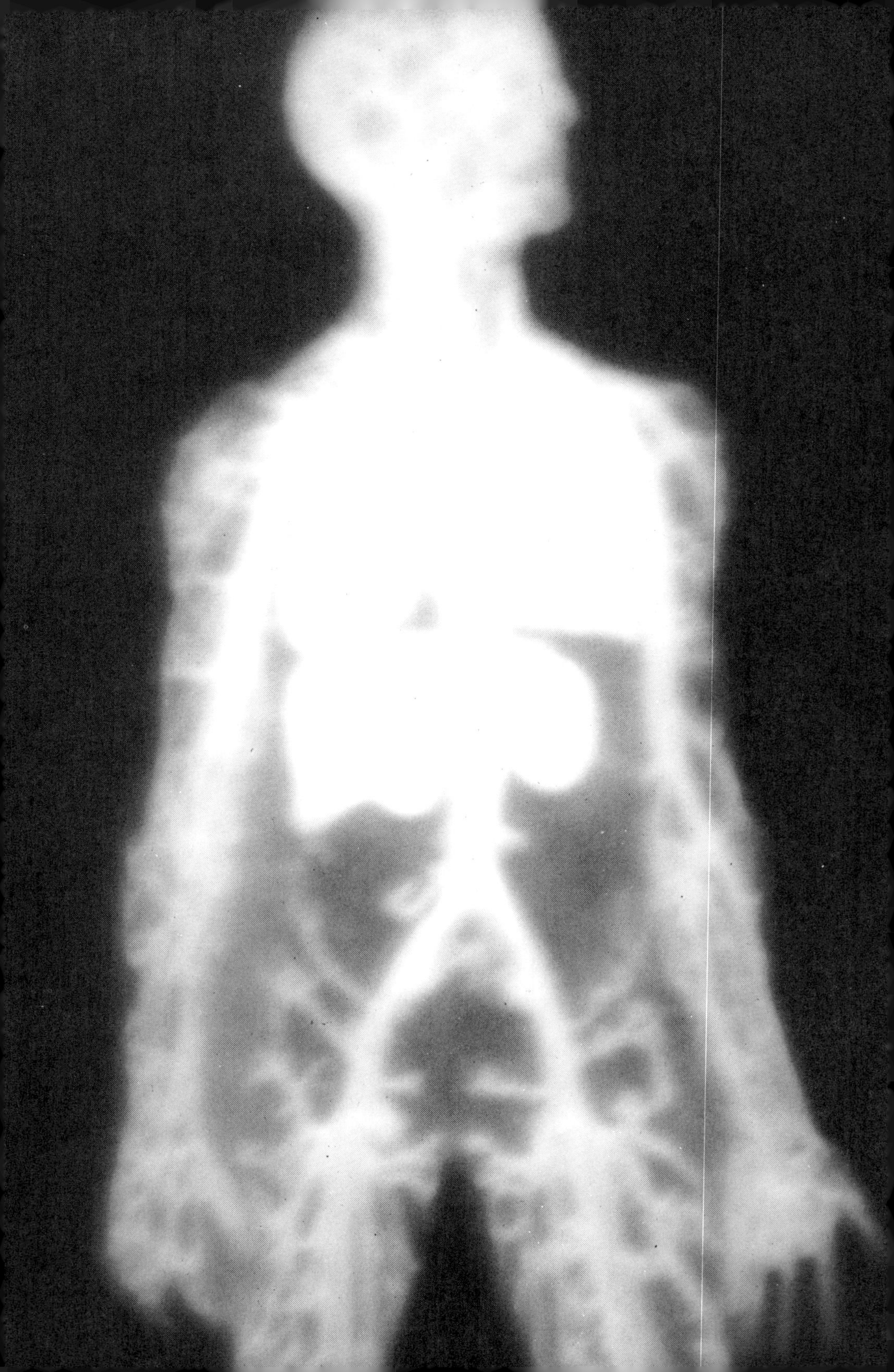

*The proper study
of mankind is man.*
       POPE

All at once, a great many things began to make sense to me and for the first time I began to truly 'see' the pattern and the *simplicity* of that pattern.

                    *   *   *

As I have stated, previously in other parts of the book, people who either 'die' and return—or people who have out-of-body experiences become 'altered' and are never the same afterward. They are much calmer—more aware of life—more empathetic towards other people—and, in general, are much better human beings because of these experiences.

Above all, they possess the comforting knowledge of exactly what will happen after they 'die' and, since the fear of 'death' no longer cripples them—they are able to lead richer, healthier and more meaningful lives.

Faith and love are apt to be spasmodic in the best minds. Men live on the brink of mysteries and harmonies into which they never enter and, with their hand on the door latch, they die outside.

R.W. EMERSON—Letter to
 Thomas Carlyle, March 12, 1835

chapter 6

the psychic world

Halicarnassus, an ancient city in Asia Minor is famous for two reasons. The first reason is that it is the site of one of the seven wonders of the ancient world—the Tomb of Mausolus, erected by Queen Artemisia in 350 B.C.

The second reason is that it was the birthplace of a remarkable man named Herodotus. What is unique about this Persian, born five centuries before the birth of Jesus of Nazareth, is that he spent his entire life in a patient, systematic investigation of virtually every nation in the world.

At the age of 20, armed with a superb education and apparently unlimited funds, he embarked upon a journey that would last for 17 years.

During that time he obtained, at first hand, factual evidence relative to the geography, climate, antiquities and monuments of each nation and—even more importantly—carefully observed the manners, morals, customs and beliefs of the people of each of these nations.

Although he deserves to be called "The Father of History"—"First Investigative Reporter" would be more fitting because of the care he exercised in reporting: "This they told me," and "This I saw happen." It's a rare trait.

The result of his labor was a vast History which was translated, eventually, into every language; was read and re-read by scholars for thousands of years; was derided, defended and disputed, generation after generation until the present day. Recently, thanks to new archeological discoveries, much of his work has been confirmed as factual.

One of the unique aspects of his work is the insight he provides into the 'psychic world'—a world that was as ancient to him as he is to us, some 2,500 years after his voyages.

His references to the 'oracles' is of particular interest to us. An oracle is a special place where, it was believed, a 'god' would respond directly (or thru the medium of a specially trained priest or priestess) to any question that was asked. The word 'oracle' incidentally is derived from the Latin word oraculum—to speak.

Although oracles were employed by the leaders of virtually every nation of that part of the world from primitive times to the relatively civilized era in which Herodotus lived, it was the Greeks who raised the custom to a fine art. Their most famous oracle—at Delphi—is familiar to any student.

What is most interesting is the inescapable fact that in almost every case that has been recorded, the oracle spoke the truth—which in most cases was not what the questioner wanted to hear.

Those questioners were no different than the people who seek advice today. They aren't interested in the *truth*—they want confirmation that what they intend to do will succeed—and that they are right in doing it.

The more things change, the more they remain the same.

The psychic world, which we will explore in this chapter is not 'supernatural', as we have been led to believe. On the contrary, it's a natural part of the total reality that Man has had access to almost from the moment he was able to think independently.

How and in what manner Early Man first perceived the psychic world is unknown to us. The few skulls that have been found only give us an indication of the *size* of the brain Early Man employed. The gray matter of the brain is not available to us. Not that it would make a great deal of difference since the brain of Modern Man (which is readily available) is still, at this late date, a mystery to science. Vast portions of the brain are as unexplored as Uranus. It has been established that a considerable part of Man's brain can be cut away and Man would continue to function in a normal manner.

Since we cannot test or question Early Man directly our only recourse is to seek understanding of his capabilities through an examination of his activities, customs and beliefs. Archeologists have unearthed tons of 'hard' evidence ranging from fossils, fragments and artifacts to entire cities, during the past two centuries. Patient piecing together has produced a remarkable comprehensive picture of Man's activities on this planet during the past ten thousand years. More recently, the work of several dedicated anthropologists has permitted us to view Man's activities as early as fifty thousand years ago.

We are now fully aware of Early Man's considerable preoccupation with 'magic' and 'gods'. Unfortunately there is a tendency, in the scientific community, to consider this simply as the activities of ignorant savages. It was Early Man's appalling ignorance, we are told, that led him to ascribe god-like attributes to any and all puzzling phenomenon.

Scientists have patiently and systematically 'exposed' the 'delusions' of Early Man by providing 'explanations' of the 'natural' phenomenon which surrounded and baffled our 'childish' and primitive ancestors.

That isn't to say that our scientists have explained all phenomena—they haven't. Not that it matters really, because what they cannot explain they tend to ignore. It's much easier that way.

One of the most important things our scientists have never bothered to explain is why primitive Man felt compelled to assign magical properties to these unknown forces in the first place.

Early Man was in no position to engage in philosophical contemplation. His primary concern was to stay alive in a hostile environment. It was a simple world. Live or die; eat or be eaten; drink or die of thirst; stay warm or freeze to death.

The basics are simple. They still exist, just as they always have—for *animals*.

Early Man was no longer an animal. He had a higher destiny from the moment he came into being. He had to investigate the psychic world because *he knew that it existed.*

How do we know that? We know because Early Man left a large body of evidence that clearly points to much more than his *preoccupation* with the psychic world; he left evidence that he *understood* it, as well.

What kind of 'evidence' did he leave behind? Astonishing evidence that demonstrates a degree of sophistication that clearly belies the terms 'childish', primitive and 'ignorant' which scientists have applied to his activities.

An immense collection of Early Man's works of art—brilliantly conceived paintings, carvings, sculpture and symbolic images has been uncovered. There is little doubt, after viewing this material, that Man firmly believed there was a link between himself and the beings who inhabited the psychic world.

His creation of a half-animal, half-Man god is an extremely sophisticated creation. It is a concept so powerful, so illuminated that it staggers the mind that it could have been created by Man at all.

Here, in this vivid, unforgettable portrait, we see the creation of a bridge between two worlds. This is a fantastic leap into the unknown which, if you think about it, makes our modern day leap into space a puny effort in comparison.

The scientific world of today, armed with a fantastic array of modern tools and technologies, takes a trip to the Moon. This is a physical trip, in a physical world from one piece of 'matter' to another.

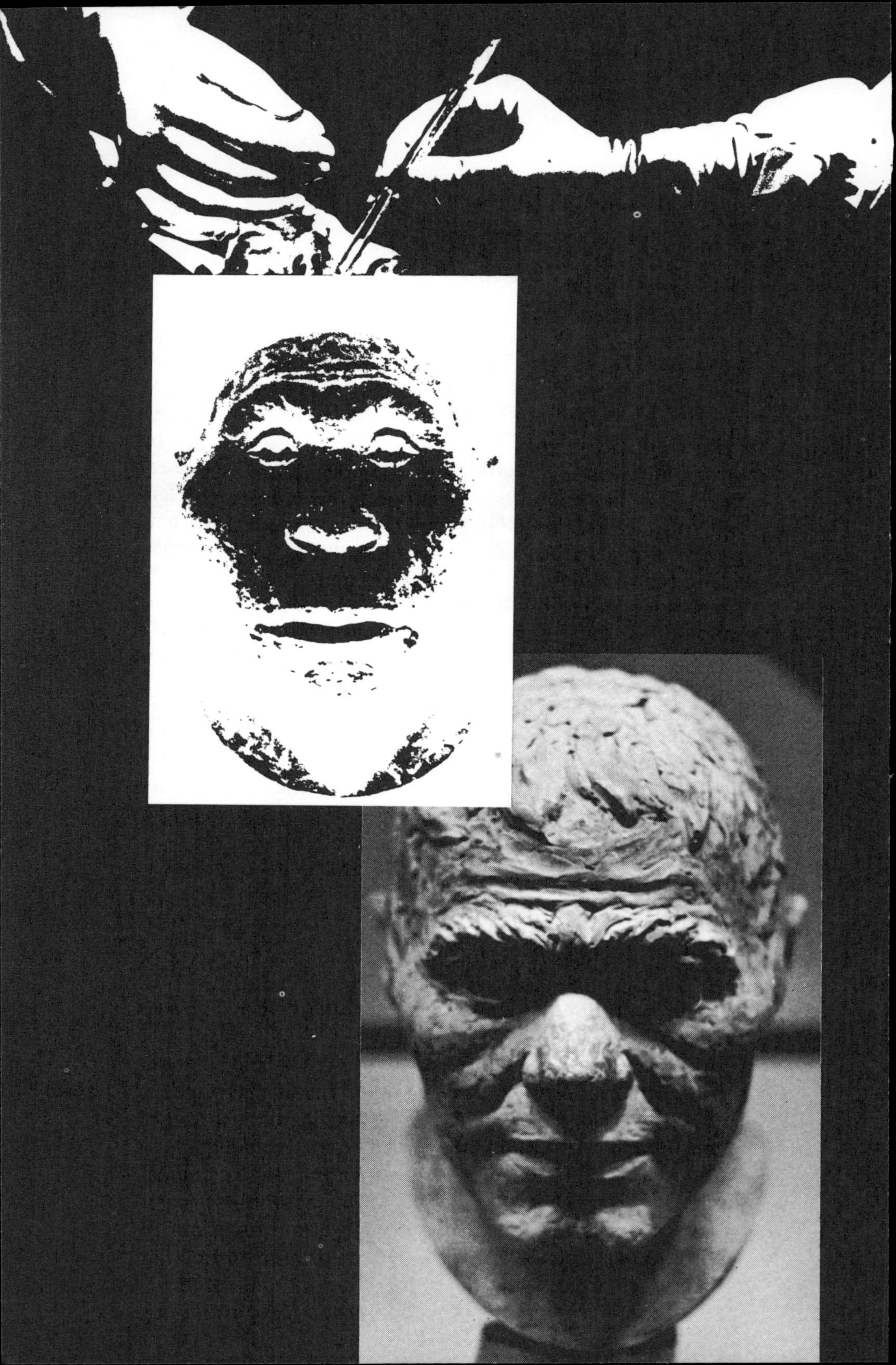

Man, made of the dust of the world, does not forget his origin; and all that is yet inanimate will one day speak and reason. Unpublished nature will have its whole secret told.
            EMERSON

On the other hand, we have primitive Man, armed only with an altered brain, alone, unaided by anything resembling a technology—without any previous experience—who dares to leap, in a single bound, from a simple, physical world, to a vast, complex psychical world.

And he succeeds!

Indeed—his bold venture changes the world from that moment forward. The bridge has been built. The road has been opened and from that moment forward there will be men who will travel that road.

The men who took that road, down through the centuries, were few in number but the gifts they brought back had an incredible effect upon billions of people in the future.

What were those gifts? Not knowledge, certainly—but rather wisdom, for as Baltasar Gracian said,

"Knowledge without wisdom is double folly."

They brought back, above all, wisdom.

"Wisdom is not an art that may be learned, wisdom comes from the stars." That's the way Paul Flemming put it, and it strikes close to the mark.

Wisdom doesn't come from the stars—it comes from the psychic world that surrounds us on all sides. That has surrounded us since the beginning of time.

When primitive Man created that bridge to the psychic world and used it—not only was he changed—but the world he lived in was changed—drastically.

Can you possibly conceive of the courage it must have taken to make that voyage into the unknown?

The men who did so, and returned, were no longer ordinary men. They were changed. They had seen and experienced what no men had seen and experienced before them. To ordinary men these changed men were as gods.

These changed men had a higher order of consciousness. They were capable of 'seeing' so much more than ordinary men and this ability was marked.

This marked change induced fear in ordinary men. They were quite right in their assumption that these marked men had been changed by the gods. They were aware that the 'gods' lived in that other world (the psychic world) and, in the main, they had no wish to go there—only to 'get along with' the 'gods' and that meant 'getting along with' the emissary of the 'gods.'

The men who had 'returned'—who became the shaman the witch-doctor—the priest of the tribe now tried to perform an incredibly difficult task. It was a multiple task that included maintaining the health and well-being of the tribe; securing and transmitting knowledge to the tribe and—above all—instilling new concepts of love, morality, nobility of mind and a preparation for the life to come. A high order of complexity and one that would tax the capability of the best of men.

While some of these new members of the priesthood succeeded (to a degree) many more succumbed to the lure of 'power' which came with knowledge and somehow managed to obscure wisdom.

It was so easy to become a 'god' for them.

Most could not resist the temptation.

There are few, today, who can.

And so these 'changed' men grasped the sovereignty that was offered them. They ultimately became the 'god-kings' of the great empires of the world.

Here and there, a handful of 'changed' men spurned the riches offered by the earthly kingdoms and tried, by patient teaching—by example—by 'miracles' to explain the path that Man must take if he was to achieve his true destiny and—with rare exception—were murdered for their pain and—in the main—their words and deeds were either forgotten or 'debunked' by scientists and the like.

Yet their deeds were recorded. There were men who studied them—puzzled over them—attempted to understand what was so plainly written a child could have understood.

But they refused to believe that it was simple. It had to be complex they thought and so they *made* it complex they made it obscure—they twisted it until no one could possibly understand what had happened. *Then* they pointed to it with scorn and said, *"See? It's meaningless!"*

And lo! It *was* meaningless.

And yet the images persisted. The deeds would not lie quietly in their twisted graves. They had an uncanny way of rising up to confront Man. The miracles, too, would not stop. They erupted continuously to the distinct embarrassment of those who held the reins of temporal power.

The god-kings of Egypt (the pharaohs) and the priests of Amen-Ra held power of such magnitude that everything in, under, on or over the very land of Egypt was under their tight control. However, the corrupted animal-gods, even in their debased condition, still held the bridge to the psychic world and there were still men who would cross over and return and remain uncorrupted.

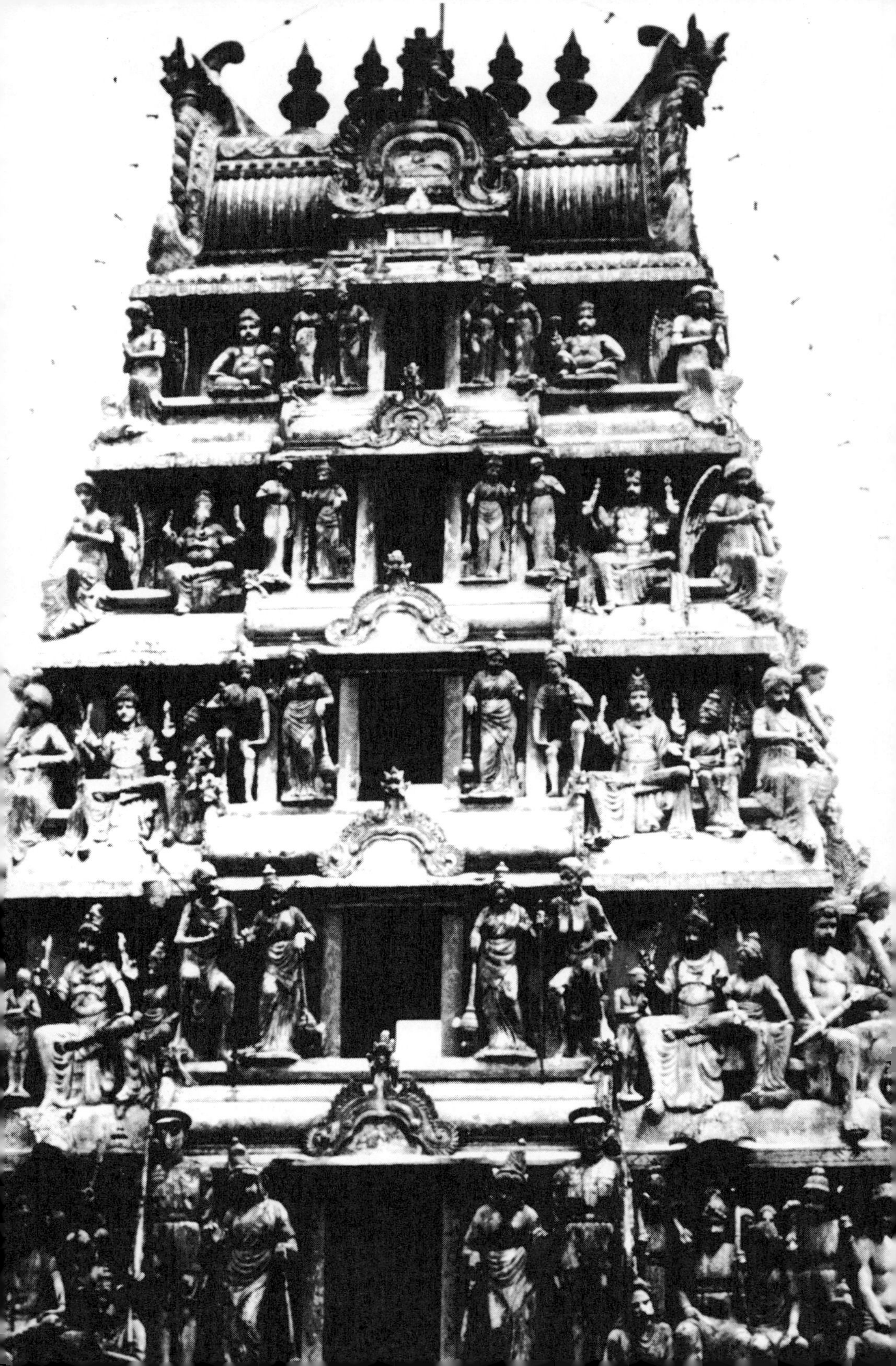

We are the music makers
We are the dreamer of dreams
Wandering by lone sea-breakers
And sitting by desolate streams
World losers and world-forsakers
On whom the pale moon gleams.
       O'SHAUGHNESSY

One of them was a young man named Amenhotep IV who, alone of all the god-kings tried to erase the terrible corruption. He changed his name to Ikhnaton (or as in some writings—Akhenaten) meaning Aten is satisfied; established the worship of a 'single' god—Aten—the Sun god, established a new capital at a place now called Tell-el-Amarna. He ushered in a new 'Amarna Age' which was stunning in its repudiation of regimes of power and corruption, of brutality and death.

He tried to establish a new order of love, justice, compassion, equality at law—in fact—a sublime order. He managed to maintain it in the teeth of the hostility of the deposed priests of Amen-Ra, for almost 20 years before it was overcome by sheer force. The conquerors tried to erase all vestige of this regime and only fragments have been found.

Enough remains—some correspondence, written on tablets—letters to the Kings of Babylon and the Kings of the Mitanni—portraits of Ikhnaton and his lovely wife Nefertiti—portraits of his children—a few astonishing works of art—because the arts flourished under his regime—enough to let us know that in that sea of darkness in men's minds there were lights of reason and nobility far beyond earthly understanding.

The trickle of light continued. It was never completely stopped. During the 1,300 years from Ikhnaton's reign until the birth of Gautama, the founder of Buddhism, there were other men who crossed the bridge.

Prophets, seers, teachers, who spent their lives—not in futility, because there were those who listened and understood the message these 'changed' men brought from the psychic world beyond.

Not many, perhaps, but enough to keep alive the hope that someday there would be more who would listen—more who would understand and venture to take the journey.

One who did and then imparted such a lesson that the world has never been the same since, was Siddhartha Gautama, a noble and well-educated Indian who was born near the border of Nepal, about five centuries before the birth of Jesus of Nazareth.

Although Gautama was born in India at about the same time that Herodotus was born in Halicarnassus, he was no historian. Gautama sought and found the bridge to the psychic world and returned with wisdom that he transformed into a religious-philosophy that gripped and held the minds of millions of people throughout the eastern part of the world.

It still does, to this day, and there are many practicing Buddhists in all parts of the world including the United States in this last quarter of the 20th Century.

Yet, only a handful have crossed the bridge.

There were men who did, in the five centuries between the birth of Gautama and the birth of Jesus of Nazareth.

More seers, prophets and teachers who cried out in the wilderness of men's minds and were not heard.

Then Jesus of Nazareth began to teach, at the age of 35 and began to demonstrate by example and by 'miracles' the truth of what he taught. And the multitudes listened, but did not hear. They 'saw' but they did not see.

But the men in high places saw and heard and it frightened them—because if the mass of people 'saw and heard' truly—then the days of the mighty were numbered.

Jesus was well aware of the anger and hostility of the powerful men in the Jewish community. He knew that they—rather than the Romans—constituted the greatest threat. The Roman governor at Jerusalem, Pontius Pilate, who was the Procurator of Judea under the Emperor Tiberius, considered Jesus one of the many harmless prophets and 'messiahs' who appeared from time to time out of the wilderness.

When, after much prodding by the Pharisees, Pilate had Jesus arrested, he "*saw no harm in him*" and was puzzled at the vehemence expressed by the religious leaders in Jerusalem.

Pilate was, first and foremost, a politician. He wanted to calm the community and so, with much reluctance, he condemned Jesus to death.

Now the odd part is—that in spite of the revelations of Jesus—in spite of the truth he offered—in spite of the demonstrated 'miracle' of his *resurrection*—all that had happened might have faded away and been completely forgotten if it had not been for one man—*Saul of Tarsus*.

This unusual man—born of strict Jewish origin—a "Hebrew of Hebrews"—was also a Roman citizen—the son of a Roman citizen—his Roman name being Gaius Julius Paulus.

Although he was a Roman citizen, Saul/Paul was reared as a Pharisee—a strictly orthodox religious sect that believed implicitly in the 'letter of religious law' and—with such an upbringing it is little wonder that he considered Jesus to be a criminal heretic.

Saul also considered the little bands of *Nazarenes* that sprang up, after the death of Jesus, to be an abomination. Saul became conspicuous as the persecutor of these little companies of 'believers' in the truth of Jesus. His role as an 'inquisitor'—seeking, finding and destroying these nests of heretics—became an obsession. He said, of himself, "*I persecuted this way unto the death, binding and delivering into prison both men and women.*"

His mission carried him beyond Jerusalem, to the villages and cities of Judea and finally even beyond Palestine.

Then—while he was on his way to the city of Damascus something happened that was to not only change *his* life—but—eventually the entire world.

What happened was a revelation of such force and of such blinding illumination that it changed Saul from an implacable persecutor of the Nazarenes into a fervent *believer*.

What happened, according to Saul—as well as to many who witnessed the revelation—was that Jesus of Nazareth appeared before Saul in a great and blinding light.

He spoke to Saul—although no one but Saul heard the words—they did see the incredible illumination.

From that moment on, Saul set his feet on a path from which he never swerved up to, and including, his execution many years later in Rome.

The story of his work and the ultimate results have been thoroughly recorded and documented elsewhere—and we need not dwell on it here.

Our concern is with the inescapable fact that Jesus of Nazareth crossed the 'bridge' again and again. The fact is that it was no 'miracle' but rather a demonstration of a natural event and that it is within the natural capability of any *Homo Sapiens Sapiens*.

Which is exactly what Jesus of Nazareth tried to tell his disciples, again and again in the simplest language possible.

He told them, plainly and simply, that they could do everything he could do—all that was required was belief.

When Jesus said, "It is easier for the camel to pass through the eye of a needle than for the rich man to enter the Kingdom of Heaven,"—he was trying to tell them that the riches of Earth are only temporary illusions, not reality. That the real world was not here, in this plane of existence.

He said—over and over—that you were as he was but you could not 'see' that "there are none so blind as will not see."

When he performed 'miracles' and denied that they were miracles he spoke the truth because only the truth was in him. He grew weary of the crowd's insatiable demands for 'more miracles' because he recognized that they were as children—delighted with the entertainment rather than with the substance of what he was trying to teach them.

Even the clear demonstration of his resurrection—his many appearances after his 'death'—carried little weight beyond that of his little band of disciples. If it had not been for Saul of Tarsus, there would be little memory of Jesus.

It would have been little more than a minor incident in a minor Roman outpost—far removed from the center of the universe which was—at that time—Rome.

And what of Saul—who was to become the greatest advocate of all—and would eventually be canonized as a saint? Saul committed the gravest error of all—he made Jesus of Nazareth into the central core of his religion and thereafter it revolved around the theme that is must be *Jesus of Nazareth* that you believed in—rather than in yourself.

That the error was real can be found in the history of the church that was founded in Rome. A history that clearly tells of the corruption that must come with knowledge and power.

The history of the Holy Roman Empire is not one whit different in its rise and fall than the histories of those great civilizations under the god-kings which flourished and died in Egypt, Babylonia, Assyria, Mexico and India.

Absolute power corrupts absolutely.

That which is best, when corrupted, becomes the worst.

And the patterns in the mind persist.

The psychic world still exists. The evidence of its existence surfaces, generation after generation, like brilliant pinpoints of light in the sea of darkness that surrounds Man. These little lights are unwavering.

When we use the term 'psychic world' one of the first thoughts concerns us with the word 'ghost' which has been with us for a considerable period of time. The word itself is derived from the Anglo Saxon word 'gost' which means breath, spirit, soul. We are also aware of the many different synonyms: *specter, phantom, apparition, and shade.*

All of them, in general refer to a disembodied spirit. Odd, isn't it, that something most people scoff at, should have a fair vocabulary of its own.

Odd, too, that Man has been seeing ghosts for as long as he has been on this planet. Man still sees ghosts—and occasional has even photographed one or two in England's famous castles.

In light of our new knowledge of OOBE's (Out of Body Experiences) it is quite easy to understand the nature of a ghost. The disembodied spirit of a man—alive or dead can (and has) moved about in this plane of existence but with considerable difficulty and evidently—from the accounts we have been given—it is extremely fatiguing.

While there is clear evidence that there was considerable bogus and fraudulent activity during the heyday of spiritualism there is also evidence of considerable truth.

There have been too many incidents to discount.

Dispassionate, scientifically trained and specially talented people have gained our attention in recent years. They call themselves 'ghost hunters' and they will, for a modest fee, investigate any ghostly happenings anywhere.

In some cases, where there clearly is 'ghostly' activities, which make life unbearable for the present day owners of a house, the ghost hunters have been able to discover the 'cause' of these nightly wanderings and, in some cases, have been able to accomplish the task desired by the 'ghost' and it has never bothered to return.

In other cases, they have been baffled by the activity and the people simply had to either move out or learn to accommodate and live with the nightly ghostly activities.

Ghosts, in this day and age, are a fairly well accepted fact of life—particularly to the home owner who discovers—too late—that he has also purchased an unearthly tenant.

Usually the 'haunting' ghost is either a victim of—or a perpetrator of—some horrible crime and seems to be earthbound by the memory of the terrible deed.

In the main stream of the psychic world, ghosts play a much smaller part than do odd and inexplicable incidents which can have no explanation in earthly terms or science.

The incidents which provide clear evidence of the existence of a psychic world have been recorded by Man since the advent of language.

In the beginning, these incidents were held in the mind of the elders of the tribe; passed from generation to generation by the spoken word; later—when writing came into vogue—these incidents were written down and remained for Man to puzzle over—to dispute—to twist and distort—which has been done.

In later years—as the incidents persisted—there came into being certain psychical societies whose aim was to record carefully and dispassionately those incidents which defied 'natural' explanation.

Their aim was to bring together a 'collection' of these incidents, each of them attested to by men and women of character and reputation.

They sought and found testimony that had been fully recorded by many of the most famous men and women in history. Kings, queens, artists, writers, soldiers, presidents, musicians and religious leaders.

To list all of the names would impose difficulties because it would require volumes but to provide some indication here are a few—in alphabetical order:

Susan B. Anthony	Jeanne D'Arc (St. Joan)
David Belasco	Samuel Johnson
Edward William Bok	Ben Jonson
Charlotte Bronte	Immanuel Kant
Robert Browning	John Knox
Luther Burbank	Abraham Lincoln
Samuel Clemens (Mark Twain)	Sir Oliver Lodge
Chauncey Depew	Martin Luther
Charles Dickens	General George Pickett
General John Fremont	Plato
General Garibaldi	Pliny
Johann Goethe	John Ruskin
Oliver Goldsmith	Charles Saint-Saens
Ulysses S. Grant	George Sand
Sir Rider Haggard	Sir Walter Scott
Edward Everett Hale	Percy Bysshe Shelley
Oliver Wendell Holmes	Socrates
Daniel Home	Emanuel Swedenborg
Harry Houdini	Alfred Tennyson
Victor Hugo	Tertullian
William James	Walt Whitman

This is only a partial list and obviously I have chosen those names which would be almost immediately recognized. For a more complete list—plus a description of the unique psychic incidents, I would recommend that you read:

"*Noted Witnesses for Psychic Occurrences*" by Walter Franklin Pierce. It's published by University Books, Inc. and the copyright is held by the Boston Society for Psychic Research. You might also contact that organization for more information about the psychic world.

At this late date in our history, there is little doubt in most people's minds that a psychic world does exist. We have viewed too many events—documented events—been presented with too much evidence—undergone too many personal experience to be able to deny the psychic world's existence. We have, for example, seen the evidence produced by Dr. Rhine at Duke University. Clear evidence that man's brain is capable of many extra-sensory performances that do not fit the purely physical world we live in.

Your brain is not what you think it is. It was designed to do much more than merely take care of the physical needs of your body or to permit you to travel about this world in safety.

Your brain contains a pattern of images—a pattern we are only beginning to understand. There is also a strong memory trace of other lives you have lived on this Earth. Above all, there is another portion of your brain which does not exist solely in this dimension but spans other dimensions.

It is this 'other' portion of your brain which permits you—on occasion—to experience what happens after death—while you are still alive.

We are going to discuss how that 'other' portion of your brain was created in the next chapter.

*Man is a darkened being;
he knows not whence he comes
nor whither he goes; he knows
little of the world and least of himself.*

GOETHE

chapter 7

the visitors/ufo's

Dr. Carl G. Jung, one of the associates of Sigmund Freud, who is recognized as one of the most brilliant thinkers in the field of psychology and psychiatry had something to say on the subject of images...

"Do we ever understand what we think? We understand only such thinking as is a mere equation and from which nothing comes out but what we have put in. That is the manner of working of the intellect. But beyond that there is a thinking in primordial images—in symbols that are older than historical man; which have been ingrained in him from earliest times, and, eternally living, outlasting all generations, still make up the groundwork of the human psyche. It is possible to live the fullest life only when we are in harmony with these symbols; wisdom is a return to them. It is a question neither of belief nor knowledge, but the agreement of our thinking with the primordial images of the unconscious. They are the source of all our conscious thoughts, *and one of these primordial images is the idea of life after death.*"

When Dr. Jung spoke about..."primordial images, symbols older than historical man..."—he was speaking directly to the point of what we have been discussing...

A pattern of images in the mind of Man.

The images are there, make no mistake about it. They are firmly implanted in the mind of Man—and only in Man—no animal possesses that unique pattern.

Just *Homo Sapiens Sapiens.*

Now the question arises: *Where did those images come from?* They are not the result of spontaneous generation like fruit flies from rotting fruit.

Those images came to Earth in the minds of other beings from another star system.

In other words, in the minds of extraterrestrial visitors to our planet.

Ten years ago, that statement would have been labeled 'science-fiction', even though a considerable number of highly intelligent, working scientists would have agreed with it—but only in private. Few of them were willing to risk the public scorn the 'authorities' heaped upon any statement concerning 'visitors from outer space', or UFO's—or anything else that departed from the comfortable assurance that Earth was the only place where intelligent life existed.

A man with a highly original mind and a gift for writing by the name of Erich Von Daniken helped to remove some of the barriers imposed by the 'closed mind' of 'authorities'.

Some of the barriers—not all—because there is still a serious battle of the minds being waged by our highly conservative establishment.

Some insight into the mentality of these conservatives may be gained from their objection to Von Daniken's work.

Why do they object to him? Because he's self-taught. He does not have a long string of college degrees behind his name. He is not a member of any acceptable scientific establishment. Therefore—by implication—his work is completely unacceptable to them.

This—in spite of the dazzling array of hard, factual material that he assembled in his brilliant book "CHARIOTS OF THE GODS?" and his equally impressive "GODS FROM OUTER SPACE" which have been translated into every language and read by hundreds of thousands of people in virtually every country in the world.

The narrow, biased judgment of the establishment has been ignored by the people, as it should be. The gates of reason, once opened, are impossible to close.

With each passing day, following the publication of Von Daniken's work, new evidence came to light. Material that had been long suppressed—hard facts relative to UFO activities, particularly in relation to our space program, began to surface. We began to hear from newsmen, like Walter Cronkite, who now admits that they were in possession of many facts relative to UFO activities but were pressured by the 'authorities' to refrain from publishing that material.

There is no way to stop this evidence from coming to light. There is too much of it. There are too many people who have seen it and want to talk about it.

Most recently we have seen the publication of a book called "*The Sirius Mystery*" by the American scholar, Roger K. Temple who has *all* the proper credentials including a well deserved fellowship, in the prestigious Royal Astronomical Society of London, which should satisfy even the most conservative member of the scientific community.

What is the "Sirius Mystery" about? It's about a tiny star called Sirius B. that has lived in obscurity because it could not be seen, even with highly sophisticated telescopes because of its proximity to the light shed by Sirius. It was finally 'seen' by means of complex telescopic photography.

Why all the fuss? Well Roger Temple spent eight years in highly intensive study of a small tribe of primitive Africans—the Dogons of Mali—because these primitive people knew all about Sirius B. They knew everything about this remarkable little star; knew exactly where it was in the heavens; knew that it was tiny but incredibly dense—a cubic foot weighs about 2,000 *tons*—which is fantastically dense. They also knew the exact shape of the orbit of this star.

This would be remarkable in itself but it then became evident that they had this highly accurate information in their possession for about 5,000 years!

Temple found that these tribesmen had stone carvings which showed the exact orbit of Sirius B. and analysis of the carvings date them at least 1,500 years old.

These primitive tribesmen had something else that was even more impressive. They had carvings which depict the 'visitors' who told them all about Sirius B. These carvings—and some drawings and paintings show the 'visitors' to be a fish-like man with a mouth and breathing holes (or slits) in the area of the chest just below the collarbone.

The tribesmen told Temple that the 'visitors' talked about their 'star system' which was based around Sirius B. They described and drew the star's orbit and location in the universe in relation to Earth.

Temple's research eventually led him to the discovery that there were Egyptian and Babylonian artifacts which also contained material similar to those held by the Dogon of Mali. Artifacts which also described the orbit of Sirius B. and the 'visitors' from that star system.

Temple's thesis—that intelligent beings from the Sirius B. star system have visited the earth many times and have exerted an influence on many civilizations like Egypt, Babylon and Nineveh has gained wide acceptance from many recognized anthropologists and astronomers.

Earth has been visited by many different peoples from many different star systems in the past 100,000 years. We are obtaining hard evidence to support that statement every day.

This is not a new idea. Long before Erich Von Daniken published his astonishing books, there was considerable disagreement, within the scientific community, as to the actual origin of works like the great pyramids of Egypt and Mexico.

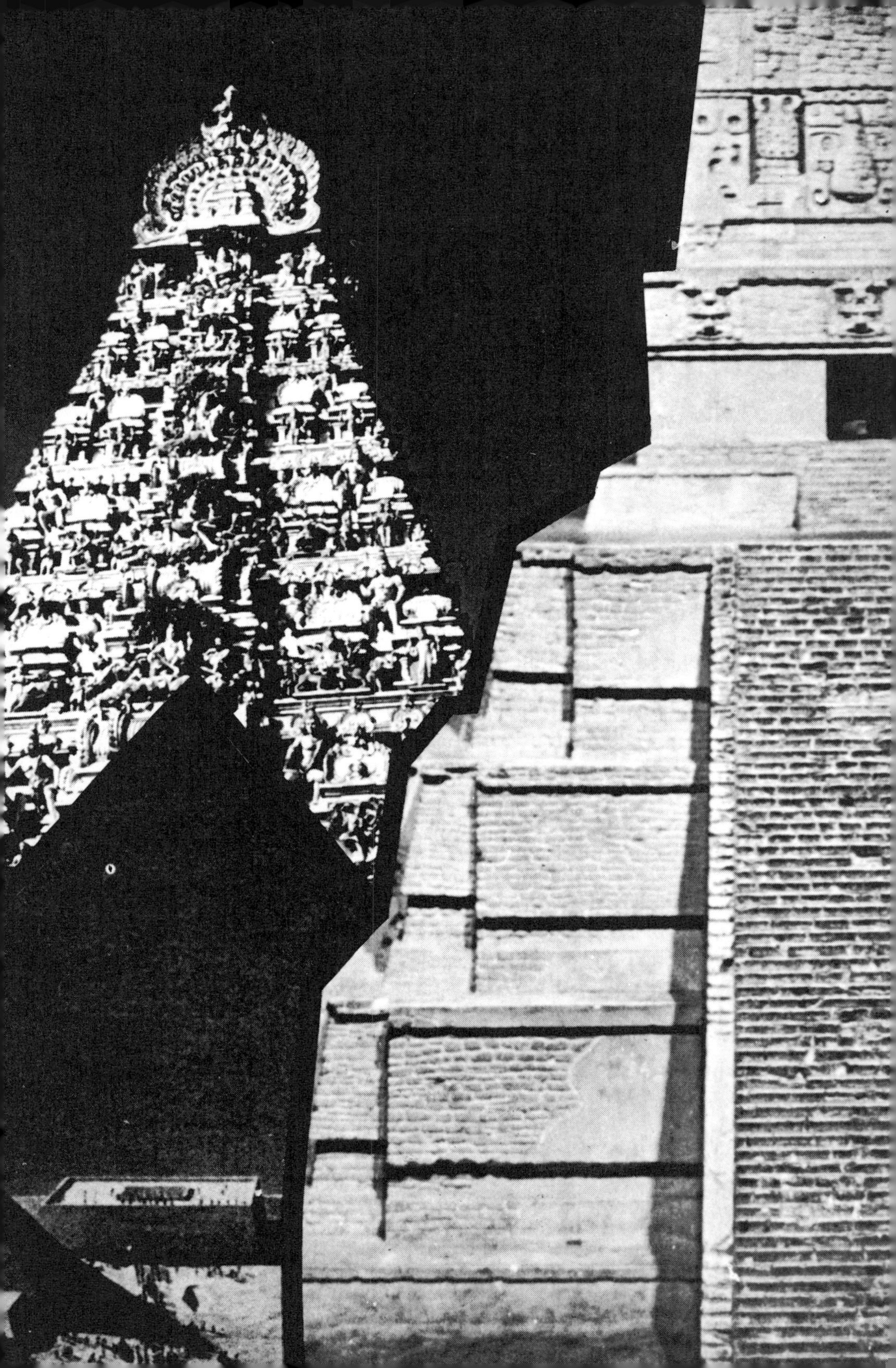

*The pyramids themselves,
doting with age
have forgotten the
name of their founders.*
   FULLER

   No one, who has not visited these immense, mathematically precise constructions, can possibly appreciate the incredible difficulties they would impose upon any civilization which attempted to build them.

   Even at *this* stage in our technological development *we* would have extreme difficulty with such a construction. It is doubtful that *we* could match the precision of these works with all of our modern equipment.

   Yet, we are expected to believe that the ancient Aztecs and Egyptians, with a technology so primitive that they didn't even have the wheel, could possibly have erected these monumental works of mathematical precision.

   There is only one way they could have been created and that is by a race of super-intelligent beings with a technology that is still light years beyond our present day technology.

   Beyond that, we still have no idea of *why* they built them at all. We will probably never know the reason. What we do know is that they were built—thousands of years before there was anything resembling a true civilization in Egypt.

   They are still standing there—mute testimony to an incredible ability that we still do not possess. As baffling as they are, they are only part of the great body of work created by these visitors from outer space.

   If you have read Von Daniken's books then you have seen the photographs of many of these incredible works some of them at least 100,000 years old.

   Nothing on Earth created those works.

   Certainly not Homo Erectus who didn't even have a decent 'opposing thumb' at the time.

   The only possible creators were super-intelligent visitors from another star system

They did a lot more than just create an enormous body of colossal works for us to gape at for thousands of years. They left behind a much more important creation. They left an altered species—*Man*.

Let's try a logical approach to what may have happened back in the dim reaches of our planet some 100,000 years ago when our first visitors arrived.

We can safely assume that Earth's first visitors were members of a scientific expedition. We can also assume that they acted in much the same manner as our scientists act as they continue our present-day expeditions to the various planets.

Earth's visitors must have taken samples of the soil, the plant life, obtained specimens of sea life and land animals—much as our scientists would have done if they had discovered life on any of the visited planets.

We can also assume that these visitors were highly intelligent and certainly possessed an extremely advanced technology. We can assume that because these visitors had solved the problems relative to *interstellar space travel*.

Remember, our technology has been barely able to solve the problems relative to travel within our own solar system. Those problems are child's play compared to the problems involving interstellar space travel.

Let's take the matter of the problems involved in traveling to the nearest star system. That would be Alpha Centauri which lies at a distance of 4.3 light years from Earth. That means if we had the ability to construct a spaceship that could travel at the speed of light—which is about 186,000 miles per *second*, it would take 4.3 years to arrive at Alpha Centauri.

However we do *not* have that capability. With our present capability and technology we *might* be able to make the trip to Alpha Centauri in 75 years. Thus, the round trip—if we didn't get out to stretch our legs—would take 150 years.

Our visitors had a very advanced technology.

They had something else on their side. They obviously had a much longer life span than ours. They stayed here for a time and made a number of trips back and forth.

Now, at some point, during their fact-gathering expedition, they must have decided upon an unusual course of action with regard to the primates.

What they did was even more incredible than the voyage they must have taken to get here.

They decided to *alter* the structure of the brain in a particular primate. It was probably Homo Erectus. Why? Because we know that something astonishing happened to *Homo Erectus* that cannot be explained in terms of evolution.

There is no doubt that our anthropoid ancestors were the result of process of evolution that took place over a period of approximately 100 *million* years.

Homo Erectus became *Homo Sapiens* almost *overnight* (in terms of evolutionary time span). In essence a new, and different kind of brain suddenly appeared and *Homo Erectus*—an animal, suddenly turned into *Homo Sapien*—a *thinking human.*

The only possible way for the new brain to have come into being was by means of an operation in which the brain was *restructured.* That kind of an operation could only have been performed by beings with an incredibly advanced science.

Our visitors from outer space had that capability.

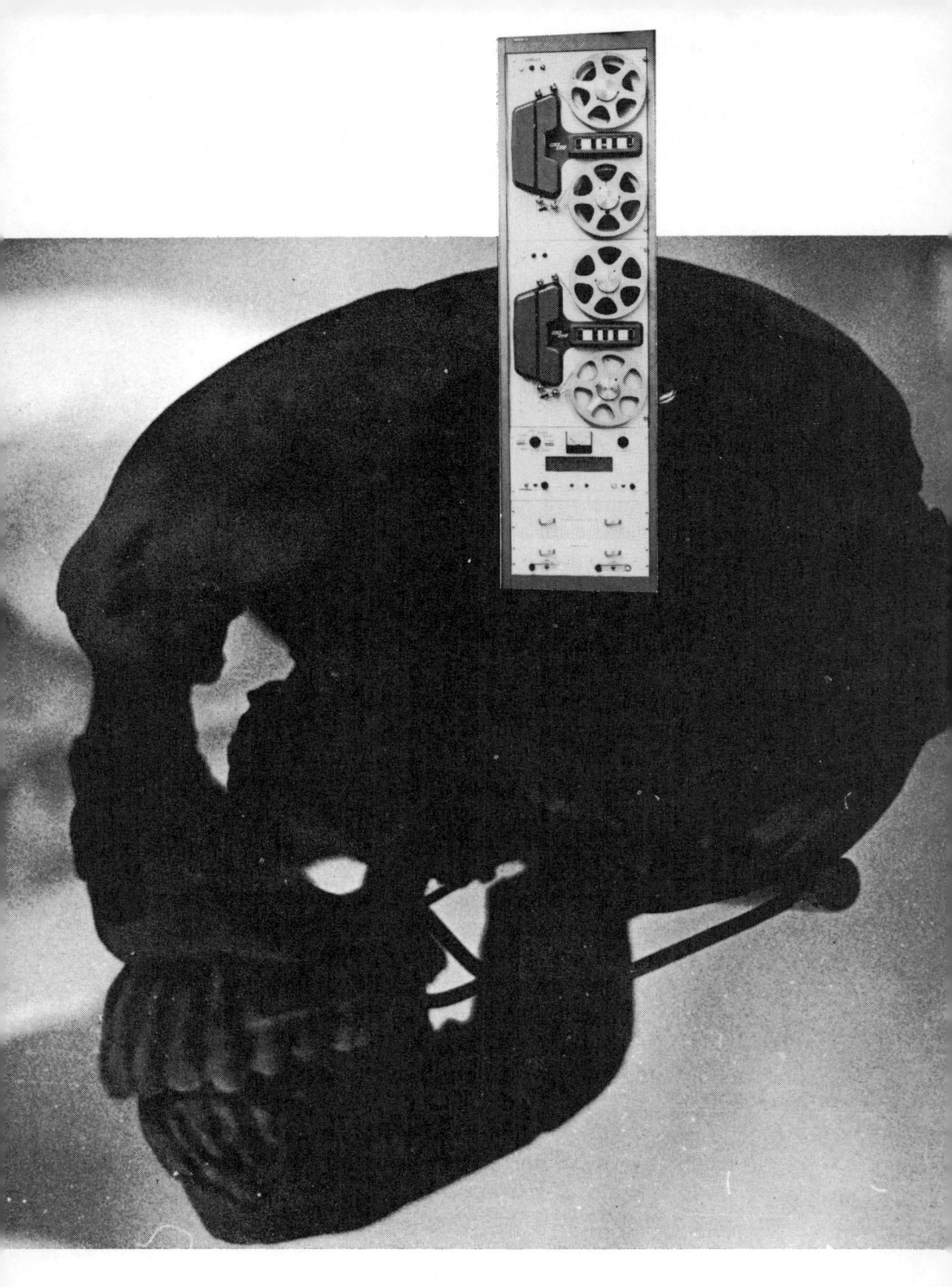

*There are three kinds of brains: one understands of itself,
another can be taught to understand, and the third
can neither understand of itself or be taught to understand.*
                    MACHIAVELLI

There is no way of knowing exactly how this unique operation was performed—whether it was a surgical operation or done genetically—we have no way of knowing.

We do know that this new brain enabled *Homo Sapiens* to do something that no animal has ever done—or ever will do—and that is it enabled Man to 'see' pictures in his mind of objects and situations *that did not exist*!

The new brain enabled Man to 'see' a picture of a particular 'shape' which, if imparted to stone or wood could create a 'tool' which would help him to perform a particular task easier and more accurately.

Once he had visualized the shape of the new tool the rest was simple. He then made a tool from wood or stone based upon his mental blueprint.

No animal will ever be able to do that.

We have seen chimpanzees use bits of wood, straw or stone as an implement but we have never seen any animal fashion a tool from any material.

The new brain also gave Man an ability to 'see' possible situations in his mind. It also permitted him to 'see' certain course of action with regard to those 'possible' situations.

It was this special ability to 'see' that contributed to Man's ability to survive in a world were he was, in every other respect, inferior to his competition for food and water in an extremely hostile environment.

Armed with that special brain, Man began to create something that had never existed on Earth before. He began to create a primitive technology.

The tools Man created enabled him to create new and formidable weapons to defend himself against the fierce relentless competition which considered Man as a part of their regular diet.

His next extraordinary accomplishment with his new brain was to 'see' that fire could be created deliberately.

This knowledge, coupled with his technology and the rapidly expanding capabilities of his new brain made Man the first Lord of his environment.

The visitors, evidently, were not satisfied with Homo Sapiens. They wanted a better, more advanced model, so they created Homo Sapiens Sapiens.

The thinking Thinking Man had arrived on the scene.

Now the advances were even more astonishing. The new tools he created were more complex, more subtle, more sophisticated. Something else was happening. The new brain was now capable of handling new concepts—new symbols—and now culture was coming into being.

This new Man began to develop the Arts—drawing, painting, sculpture—he began to delineate the pictures in his mind. He became aware of color—of form—of motion.

Images in the mind of Man.

Now the flowering of the seed that had been implanted. Man began to be aware that the basic concept was simply that...

Anything that could be visualized could be created.

That was a giant leap forward.

Oddly enough it was not the male of the species who took advantage of that great concept—it was the female. In many respects she displayed capabilities that were more astonishing than his. She began to form concepts that would—eventually—thrust Man into Space.

It is quite possible—that if it hadn't been for the female brain—and the unique concepts it was capable of—that Man would still be living in caves—hunting and fishing as he did in the early part of his development.

It was the female of the species who first 'saw' that it was a waste of time and energy to follow the great herds as they migrated to new grazing grounds. It was more sensible to stay in place and raise food rather than chase after it. This led to farming and animal husbandry and the ultimate creation of the great city-state civilizations.

The master plan of the 'gods from outer space' was not limited to survival—or a 'better way of life' for Man. They wanted Man to have more leisure so that he could 'think' of something else than how to satisfy the hunger and thirst that haunted him until he had built a civilization.

They wanted more important things to occupy his mind. These 'more important things' would begin to emerge once Man's insatiable appetite was eased. These images of 'other' dimensions—of 'other' worlds—of another life after death would begin to surface and begin to shape his thoughts away from this plane of existence as we shall see in the next chapter.

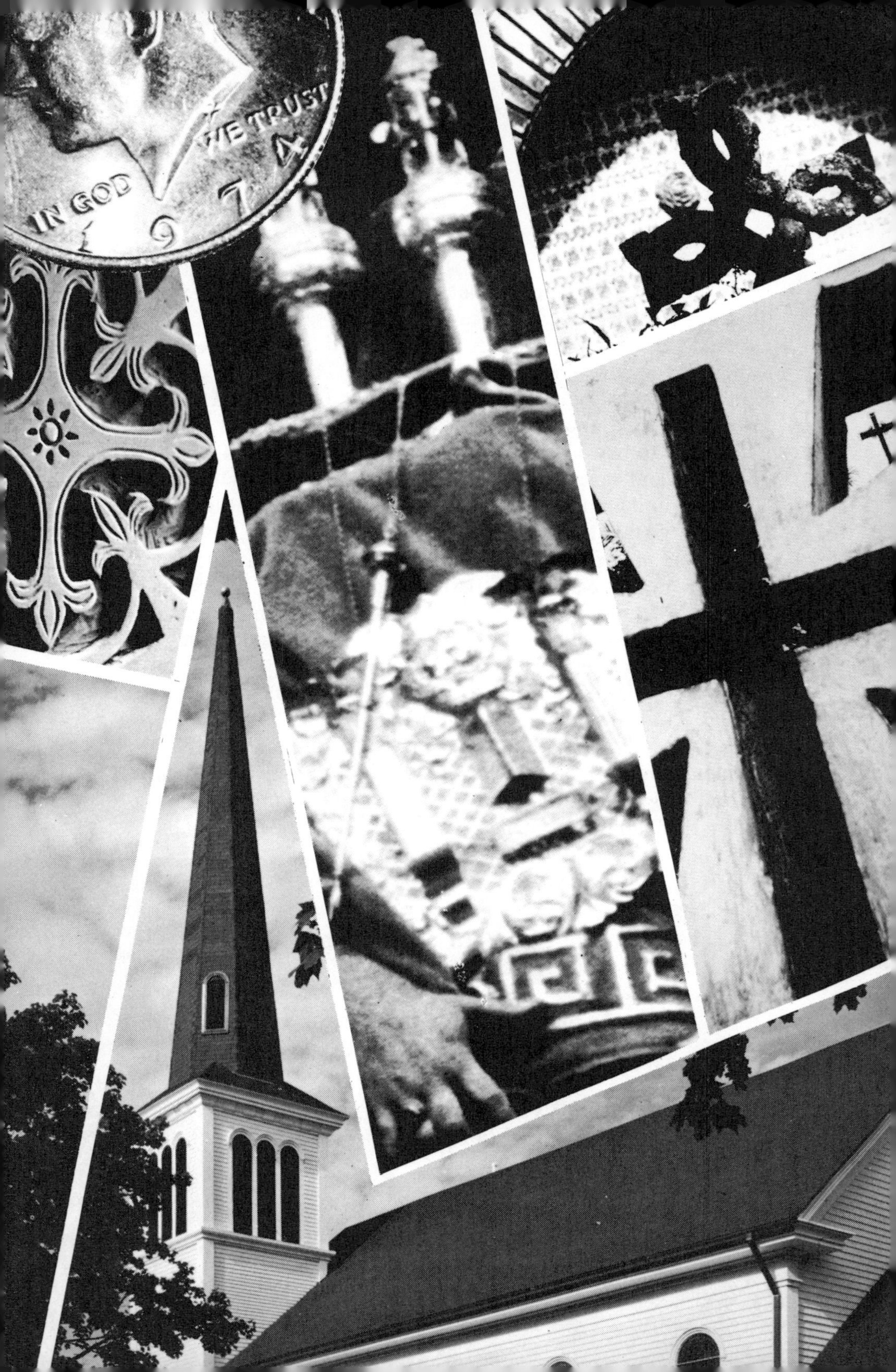
IN GOD
WE TRUST
1974

chapter 8

magic and religion

Since the masses of the people are inconstant, full of unruly desires, passionate and reckless of consequence, they must be filled with fears to keep them in order. The ancients did well, therefore, to invent gods, and the belief in punishment after death. It is rather the moderns who seek to extirpate such beliefs who are to be accused of folly.

POLYBIUS—Histories 125 B.C.

As much as I admire Polybius, that admirable and distinguished Greek historian who managed during his seventeen years of political exile in Rome, to write at least forty books—I must disagree with his notion that *the ancients created gods*.

It is the other way round. The gods created the ancient ones—or—to put it another way—it was the visit of the gods which originated magic which later helped start religion.

It would be well at this point, before misunderstanding arises, to point out that it is *not* my intent in this chapter to either oppose or defend any of the religions which exist today. I shall only ask that you read this chapter with the same degree of dispassion as I asked of you in the very first pages of this book. If you feel that you cannot—or that what you are about to read may distress you—then I suggest that you skip this chapter and move on to the next one.

I intend, in this chapter, to examine the roots of magic, mythology and religion, particularly as they pertain to the development of Man in the 30 to 40 thousand years before the beginning of recorded history. I believe that we will be able to clearly demonstrate that Early Man was fully aware of a life after death; that he left visible evidence of this knowledge, and made that knowledge part of his lifestyle.

I shall also discuss the inescapable evidence that the patterns in the mind of Early Man were implanted and they have existed from that time to the present day without the slightest change or alteration.

I shall begin with the presentation of two related pieces of factual evidence with reference to 'implanted' images.

Thanks to the combination of high-speed photography and the medium of television, millions of people have been able to see, at first hand, some of the astonishing events that take place almost daily in the animal and plant world on this planet.

One particular film concerns the almost incredible drama involved in the laying and hatching of the eggs of the giant sea-turtle.

The film begins in the middle of the night on a lonely island in the Pacific Ocean. We see a giant sea-turtle emerge from the sea and then drag herself awkwardly with her great flippers, a considerable distance inland.

She stops, finally, and begins to dig a hole in the sand.

Then, positioning herself over the hole she begins to lay hundreds upon hundreds of round, glistening eggs in the sandy nest. It is almost dawn when she completes her obviously exhausting task.

Now, slowly and painfully, she begins the task of covering the eggs with sand. We are fully aware of the agony caused by each movement of her giant flippers, yet she never pauses but continues to scoop the sand and deposit each bit on the next until it is completely covered to her satisfaction.

Then she begins the slow, awkward trip back to the sea and we unconsciously have the urge to help her as she inches towards the safety of the water.

Finally she reaches it and, as she swims slowly away, the narrator tells us that she will never return and never really know if her young will be born.

The second part of the drama unfolds at dawn on the eighteenth day following the laying of the eggs. There is a stirring in the sand and suddenly a young sea-turtle emerges and immediately begins to squirm across the land towards the ocean, which is a considerable distance away and cannot be seen (at this point) by the young sea-turtle.

More turtle young begin emerging from the sand and begin the awkward and difficult task of reaching the safety of the sea and now, as the camera draws back, we not only hear but *see* the hundreds of gulls that have gathered for the feast and now we know the reason for the frantic haste expressed by the young sea-turtles.

Only the strongest, swiftest (and luckiest) sea-turtles will survive the onslaught of the ravenously hungry gulls who dive, rip and tear at the defenseless young sea-turtles.

The carnage is frightful. While most of the sea-turtles make a direct line for the sea, some are confused and take the wrong direction; others turn hopelessly in wide circles. A number of them, flipped over by the gulls, waggle their flippers in a futile effort to right themselves.

When it is finally over, quiet descends upon the island and the gulls feast upon the bodies of the turtles that did not succeed in reaching the safety of the sea.

The drama, for now, is over, but it will be repeated again, on some dark night in the future, when one of the female sea-turtles who escaped, will return and lay her eggs in the warm sand on this lonely Pacific island.

Now, while you may find this interesting, as I have, you may wonder what connection it has with the subject of this chapter (Magic and Religion). Have patience, there is an important connection, which we shall discuss shortly.

In another study—that of the newly-hatched chicken, we are treated to an even more striking phenomenon. That of 'instant' recognition of a particular symbol.

We watch the young chicks break out of their shells and, at that moment, the wooden model of a hawk is 'flown' over their coop on a long wire.

The chicks run for cover instantly.

Now there would be nothing unusual in this action except that the chicks do not run for cover if the model of any other bird is flashed along the wire. The models of ducks, gulls, herons, pigeons, geese—no other bird-image will provoke the instant retreat by the chicks.

If the shadow image of a hawk moves across the ground in front of their coop they will run for cover. Not so with the shadow of any other bird.

The newly born chick, like the newly born sea-turtle, had an image implanted in its brain. In one, it was the image of a hawk—in the other—the image of the sea.

Both reacted instantly—at the moment of birth—to the implication involved in their implanted image.

Suppose that it was possible to show that Man is also born with an implanted image—or possibly a number of implanted images.

Do you recall, as a very young reader, your first encounter with the Brothers Grimm and their fabulous collection of 'fairy-tales'? I do. I can remember, as clearly as if it were yesterday, the first time I opened that fat book of stories and became 'lost' in the amazing world they opened to me.

It wasn't until many years later, while attending classes at a local university that I began to understand exactly what Jacob and Wilhelm Grimm had been up to when they began to compile that collection of folklore.

They were attempting to show the strong possibility of a direct connection between Indian and European mythology. They had no intention of providing considerable enjoyment and entertainment for succeeding generations of children around the world.

Their project was one of many scientific attempts to investigate the meaning and significance of myths and legends in various parts of the world.

They discovered more than they bargained for.

Their efforts, coupled with the new evidence uncovered by archeologists, began to lay bare a pattern of thought that seems to indicate that Man, at all times, and in all places, carried in his brain an identical set of implanted images.

Remember that, up until 1821, Greek, Roman and Judean/Christian religious literature comprised the major body of work that was accessible to scholars.

Then when Champollion succeeded—with the help of the Rosetta Stone—in deciphering the baffling Egyptian hieroglyphics, the scholastic world suddenly had access to thousands of years of literature, some of which pre-dated the Greeks and Romans by as much as three thousand years.

Within a period of ten years the myths and legends of the South Sea Islands were brought to light by William Ellis in his Polynesian Researches.

North American Indian mythology was collected and made available in 1839 by Henry Schoolcraft and six years later the astonishing city-states of Nineveh and Babylon began to come to light under the direction of Sir Henry Layard.

While the Civil War was raging, here in America, several great works were published which dealt with discoveries which ranged from proof of the existence of Man in Europe more than 100,000 years ago—to the translation of an ancient Central American mythological text.

And so it went—year after year—with discovery piled on discovery, *until an entirely new pattern of thought lay exposed for the first time.*

I'd like to try a simple experiment. It merely requires that you remember a previous experience you may have had involving extreme height. Have you ever been a passenger in a small, private plane? Have you ever stood on a mountain top on a clear day? Perhaps you can remember the first time you stood at the top of an extremely tall building—the Empire State Building or the Eiffel Tower in Paris—for example.

Now try to remember your sensation as you looked down, from that height. If you were in a small plane then perhaps you can remember the amazing regularity of the pattern created by the brown and green farmlands below you. Or, if you were flying over the city—the precision of the avenues as they crossed the city as compared to the meanderings of the main streets.

If you can remember those sensations then perhaps you can appreciate the sensation of the scholar, today, as he stands at this particular vantage point in time and is able to look back at an expanse that covers 100,000 years of Man's existence. Now, for the first time, he is able to see the clearly expressed pattern of Man's thought.

This pattern, most clearly expressed in mythology, is as vivid and impressive as the green and brown patterns of the farmlands we saw from the vantage point of that small, private airplane.

The novelist and philosopher, Thomas Mann expressed it perfectly when he said,

"The myth is the foundation of life, the timeless schema, the pious formula into which life flows when it reproduces its traits out of the unconscious."

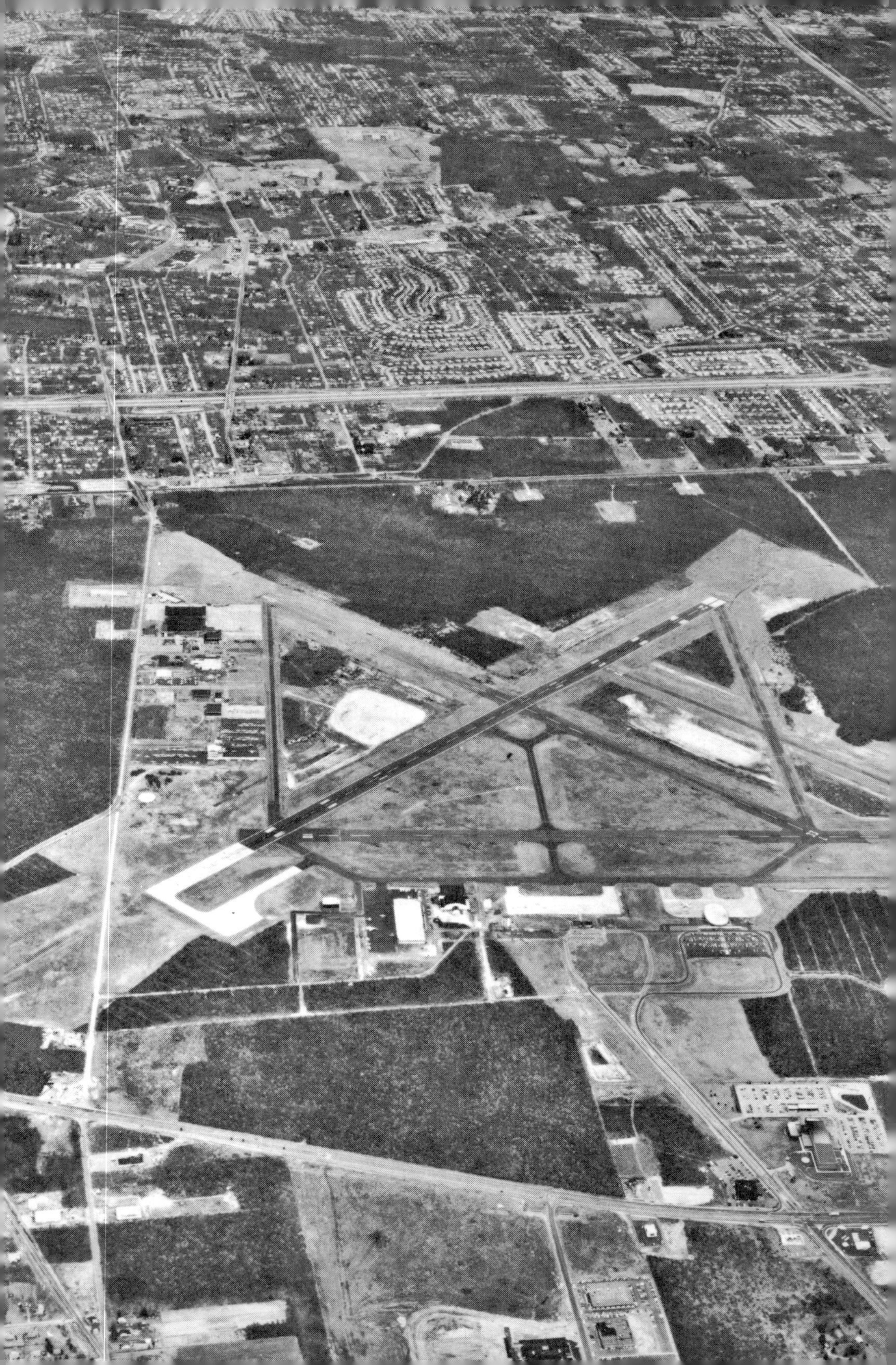

The mind, in discovering truth, acts in the same manner as it acts through the eye in discovering an object. When once an object has been seen, it is impossible to put the mind back to the same condition as it was in before it saw it.
                                    PAINE

The great truth, trapped in the shattered fragments of mythology, hidden under the dust of centuries, has now been brought to light, thanks to the life-long labor of thousands of men and women in a hundred different fields of which anthropology, archeology and psychology are only a portion of the scientific disciplines involved.

Today there is little doubt that a pattern of images has existed in Man's mind from the very beginning of Man's emergence into being.

It was that pattern of images in the mind of the Neanderthal Man which caused him to begin engaging in ceremonial burial; it was that pattern of images in the mind of subsequent Man which laid the foundation of mythology.

We now come to an astonishing piece of literature which, like truth, lay in dust-covered fragments for thousands of years prior to its discovery in the excavated ruins of Assurbanipal, King of Assyria from 668 B.C. to 626 B.C. This epic—that is to say—a kind of narrative poetry, written in an elevated or grand style, whose subject matter deals with heroic action—concerns the activities of a hero named *Gilgamesh* and his companion, a tamed, primitive man of great strength named *Enkidu*.

When the fragments were put together, it was discovered that there were twelve chapters, each one dealing with a great adventure by this pair of heroes.

The patterns or images created by this epic found their way into the mythology of the Hebrews, Phoenecians, Hittites, Syrians, thence to India; became part of Greek and Roman mythology, transversed Europe and reached into the Icelandic and Teutonic mythologies. It actually spread to every land, every peoples on the face of the Earth and—if we may go from the sublime to the utterly ridiculous—still exists today in the form of comic strip heroes like Batman and Robin—or, if you will, The Six Million Dollar Man and The Bionic Woman.

Magic was practiced by Early Man at least fifty thousand years before recorded history began. We know that because of the immense underground rooms and labyrinths which have been discovered in Spain and France. In one of these—the labyrinths in the Pyrenees Mountains in southern France, at a place called Arieges, one of the greatest collection of magical work ever created by Man was discovered. It was created by Paleolithic Man (Early Stone Age Man).

As you enter this cave you are forced, due to the peculiar construction, to crawl like a serpent through a long, dusty, tight fitting tunnel for what seems like an eternity. Then—quite suddenly—you emerge into a chamber (which must have been brightly lighted) filled with vivid paintings and carvings of virtually every kind of beast that roamed that area some forty or fifty thousand years ago.

The most awesome sight—which captures your attention immediately—is the full length portrait, in full color, of a half-man, half-animal god, high up on the wall, in a slight recess, fifteen feet above the floor of the chamber.

This half-man, half-animal god had brilliant, piercing eyes, huge antlers, ears like a stag, the paws of a bear (for hands), the legs of a man, the long bushy tail of a wolf and beneath that, the large sexual organs of a lion.

It's a vivid, impressive portrait with a power that is undimmed by the fifty thousand years it has waited in that recess in the wall.

This terrifying image of a half-man, half-animal god can be found in the magical and religious ceremonies of every nation on Earth. It has been employed by the North American Indians—the Aztecs and the Mayans—by the Egyptians—the Babylonians—Assyrians—Hittites. It has been found in the ruins of Cambodia—in India—in every corner of the world—

in every civilization of the world. It persisted for more than fifty thousand years.

And what of the labyrinth in that enormous magical complex? Can there be any doubt of the meaning? Of course it suggests ritual initiation into a tightly controlled magical society—but there is *more*.

There is the basic theme of *rebirth*. The passage in the completely darkened, tightly fitting tunnel; the fear that must have been in the mind of the initiate as he crawled slowly through this long passageway towards the *unknown*; then, suddenly, he emerges into the new and astonishing, brilliantly lighted world of the chamber.

More astonishing, more frightening, is the fact that he is suddenly face-to-face with a god from another world. He has made the journey from this plane of existence to another, higher plane of existence. He has, in essence, been re-born. He has entered another life.

Where did this knowledge of life after death come from?

How could that Early Stone Age Man arrive at such a sophisticated concept if it wasn't deliberately implanted in his new, altered brain?

The 'gods' from outer space implanted it.

They did much more than implant the knowledge of a life after death in the mind of Early Man. They also created an instrument which would permit man to visit the dimensions that lie beyond death. The instrument was in his altered brain. The vehicle was 'sleep' the sister of death.

The memories of his visits to that other dimension are called 'dreams' and that is the subject we are going to explore in our next chapter.

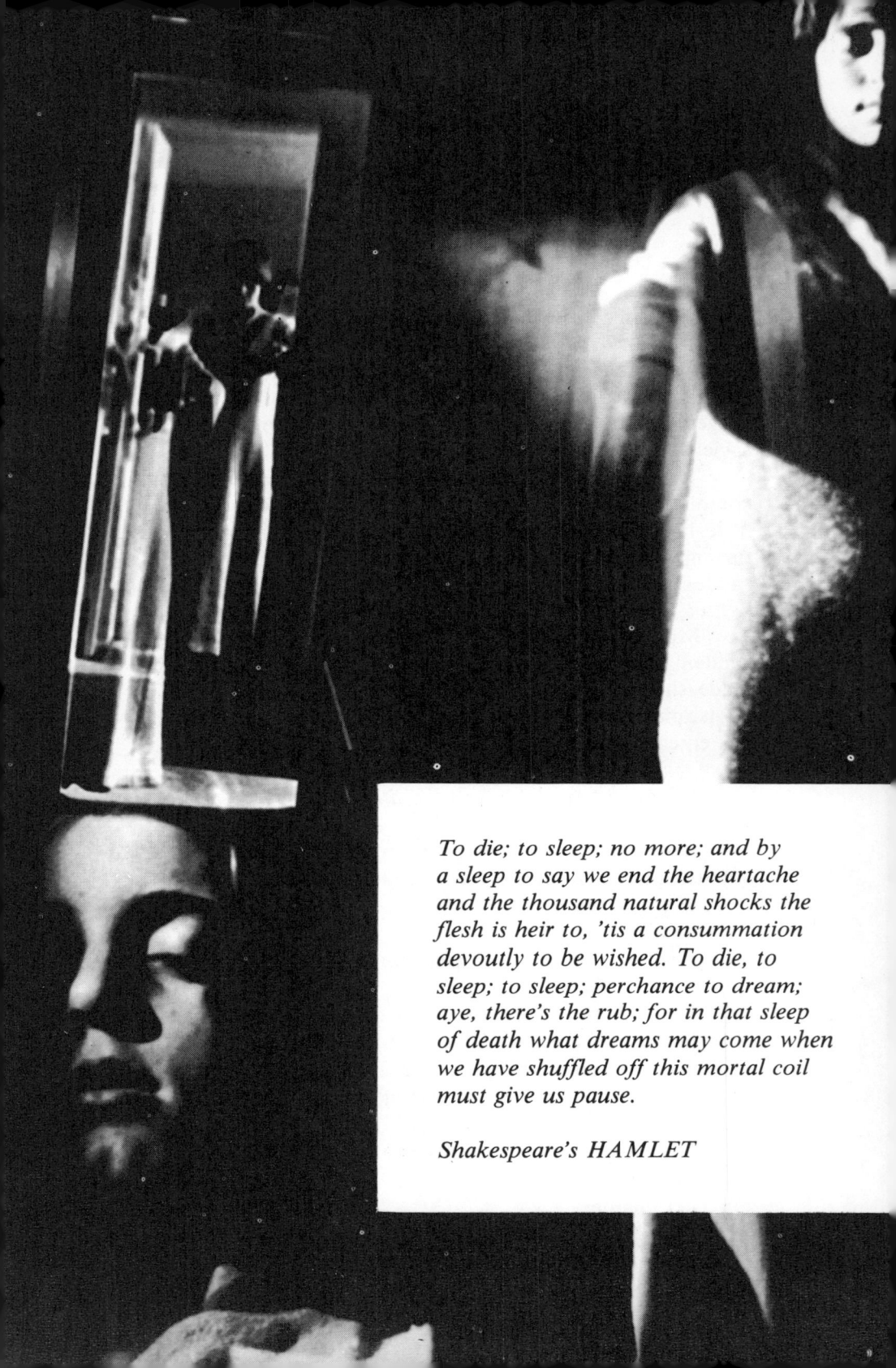

To die; to sleep; no more; and by a sleep to say we end the heartache and the thousand natural shocks the flesh is heir to, 'tis a consummation devoutly to be wished. To die, to sleep; to sleep; perchance to dream; aye, there's the rub; for in that sleep of death what dreams may come when we have shuffled off this mortal coil must give us pause.

Shakespeare's HAMLET

chapter 9

the world of dreams

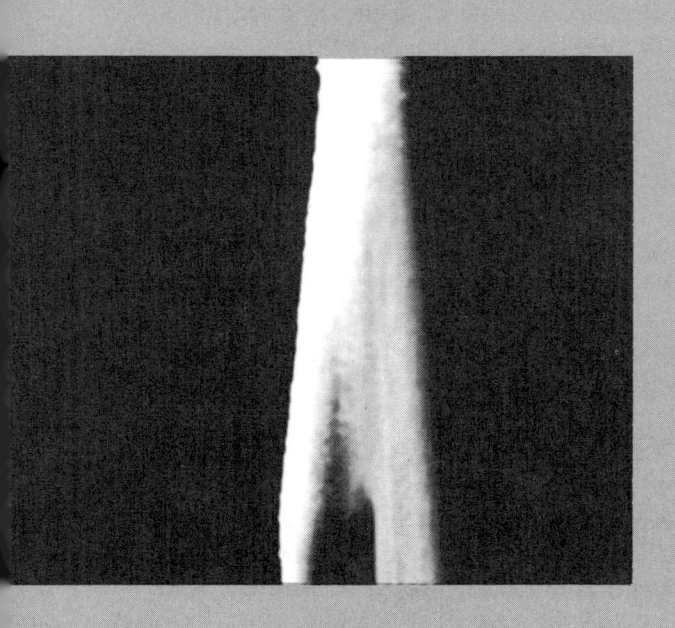

Now we are going to discuss one of the most intriguing and certainly one of the most *important* aspects of human existence—the act of dreaming—every time you sleep.

Sleep has been called many things since the beginning of Man's concern with it. Sleep has been called the 'little death'—the 'imitation of death'—the 'sister of death'—and in almost every instance there is the recognition that death and sleep have something in common. It's not at all surprising then to consider that *dreams* have also been connected with the concept of death.

The mystery that surrounds dreams has been a continuous source of fascination to Man almost from the moment of his creation. Dreams have played an important role in every society, every civilization; they have changed the course of history, contributed to the rise of magic, of religion and—eventually—to the greatest flowering of science and technology in the history of the world.

Yet the nature of dreams is still a mystery to us.

The shaman, the witch-doctor, the priests of Amen-Ra and present day scientists, collectively, managed to produce a mountain of books which speculated upon the nature of dreams but all of them, without exception, finally admitted that they just didn't know.

Greek philosophers, including Democritus, Aristotle and Pliny have given us theories that ranged from "ghosts in the atmosphere waiting to attack the soul of the sleeper" to "objects that are 'seen' by the body" to "supernatural intervention". Interesting theories but not conclusive.

And what did Hippocrates, the 'Father of Medicine' have to say about dreams? This learned scholar and physician whose Hippocratic Oath is still administered to men about to enter medical practice, believed that while dreams might be of a divine origin, it was more likely that they were either the direct result of gross indigestion or an early warning of a disease within the body.

That has a 'modern' ring to it. That's because most present day physicians tend to agree with that diagnosis (eliminating the 'divine' aspect, of course).

Rene Descartes, the French philosopher who gave the world: *Cogito ergo sum* (I think, therefore I am) believed that thought was the cause of dreams because he believed that thought was continuous in the mind of Man regardless of his waking or sleeping state.

Oddly enough, three centuries after that novel theory was presented by Descartes, we have proof that thought *is* continuous in the mind of Man. We know that the mind is always active because we have observed the activity, in a waking or sleeping state, with EEG studies (electroencephalograph studies) wherein the electrical impulses given off by the brain are magnified and then recorded as a series of wave transmissions on paper.

Further studies with REM (Rapid Eye Movements) which take place during the progress of a dream, when coupled with EEG, have enabled scientists to record human brain waves before, during and after dreams take place. The continuous record shows that the idea that Descartes presented was absolutely true. There is continuous brain activity throughout your lifetime.

The significance of this knowledge can be appreciated by considering that the only accepted medical definition of clinical death today is the complete absence of brainwaves.

Now that we have part of the facts relative to dreaming let's examine some of the current theories regarding the nature of dreams.

Sigmund Freud was—in essence—similar to Darwin in that Freud gave the world a revolutionary theory with regard to the nature of dreams that caused almost as much fuss and controversy as Darwin's claim that Man had evolved from an ape. Freud developed the idea that dreams are, in the main, an unconscious representation of repressed sexual desires. That really caused a sensation.

While I may concur—in part—with Freud's theory, I must say that I think he missed the mark. In fact most of the people who professionally investigate dreams—such as psychiatrists, psychotherapists and the like—also miss the mark by a wide margin.

They assume, for example, that all dreams deal in symbols—objects that represent something *other* than what they appear to be. There is a certain amount of truth in that. However it would be more accurate to say that a dreamer sometimes uses symbols to disguise the true nature of his dream.

That's because it happens, quite often, that a dreamer will have a perfectly 'straight' dream—usually of a future event (clairvoyance) and there isn't a symbol in sight; it's just a perfectly straightforward dream.

Why the use of symbols then?

There are times when we do have a deep feeling about something we have done—or want to do—and we have deliberately 'put it out of our mind' because we didn't want to think about it. If this happens too often the subconscious will 'throw it back at us' but will disguise the message so that it can get by the 'censor' that stands guard over our conscious mind during sleep.

Consider, for the moment, what happens when we have an OOBE (out-of-body experience) during sleep. There's no attempt to disguise it mainly *because we do not realize that it is an actual experience rather than just a 'dream'*.

Your 'built-in-censor' will not attempt to stop or erase this kind of a dream because it represents no threat to your security or peace-of-mind. Bad or violent dreams (nightmares) *do* get through because they are clothed in symbols which the censor does not believe you will be able to interpret—and it's almost always right!

You do, however, wake up highly disturbed and more often than not will attribute the 'bad' dream to something you ate just before going to sleep. That always seems like a perfectly valid piece of logic—even when you can't actually pinpoint the offending food.

It isn't really because many of your worst nightmares are really frightening OOBE's rather than just bad dreams.

Let's do a bit of investigating into this business of dreaming—particularly into your dreams. We'll start with some established facts about dreams.

Everyone dreams every time they go to sleep.

Please do not shake your head at me. Everyone—and that includes you—either dreams or has OOBE's every night of his life.

This is not an opinion or a theory. It is an established fact. Carefully controlled laboratory investigations with volunteer, human subjects have established:

1. Dreaming takes place each time a subject sleeps.
2. If the subject is *not permitted to dream* for a continuous period of time, the subject will begin to exhibit marked reactions such as pain, violent hallucinations and strong anti-social behavior.
3. If the subject was prevented from dreaming over too long a period of time—death would occur.

You may take, for an established fact, that everyone does dream each time he falls asleep; and dreaming is a vital part of human existence.

We are then faced with a question which has never, as far as I know, been answered satisfactorily. That is:

Why do you dream?

None of the current medical, psychological or psychiatric answers appear to be valid. They each hold a part of the truth but, as we said earlier, truth is not divisible.

For example: the indigestion theory—the idea that we dream because of something we have eaten that disagrees with us is not true because we dream when there is no indigestion present. Our being restricted (tangled up in a blanket)—or when we throw off the covers and are chilled—these actions do not cause dreams—they become part of the dream.

The restriction, caused by being tangled in a blanket might cause you to dream that you are tied up—caught in quicksand—pinned under something—*but never that your feet are tangled in the blanket.* So too, if you lost the blanket and become chilled, you might dream that you are lost in a blizzard—or drowning in freezing water—but never that you have lost the blanket.

The actual happening becomes an ingredient in your dream but never the happening itself.

Then we come to the most popular notion—Freud's idea that most dreams reveal repressed sexual desire. Here we have one of the most interesting theories and certainly one of the most difficult to refute because most of us do have repressed sexual desires. We live in a world that trains us from childhood to repress certain natural functions. Toilet training being the first important repression. Next in line is the natural sexual drive in children which we also curb—although not to the degree it once was repressed. It is, however, a natural inclination which is not permitted to have free expression whenever and wherever we are so moved.

The fact remains that this repression becomes an ingredient in the dream and not the cause of the dream because we dream when there is no sexual repression.

If we consider the act of dreaming without regard to 'symbols'—indigestion—restriction—or repressed sexual desire—then we are faced with a continuous human activity that has significance in itself.

Think for a moment. If you sleep or dream, on the average, about eight hours out of twenty four hours of each day, then it is apparent that you are sleeping and dreaming for *one third of your lifetime*! If you reach the age of sixty, then you will have spent *twenty years* in sleeping or dreaming. Don't you think that's important?

Aren't you curious? Wouldn't you like to know what you are doing with that part of your life? You should be because it's probably the most important part of your life.

Consider, for a moment, the case histories you read in the chapter on the Visible/Invisible World. The OOBE's which were discussed all took place during an unconscious state of being—which is another way of saying that each of those persons was asleep.

Isn't it quite possible that all of the activities that take place during sleep are simply forms of OOBE's? That your dreams are the distorted memories of those experiences? That the reason they are distorted is that you experience difficulty in understanding them because of the limitations of your conscious mind with its limited dimensional capabilities?

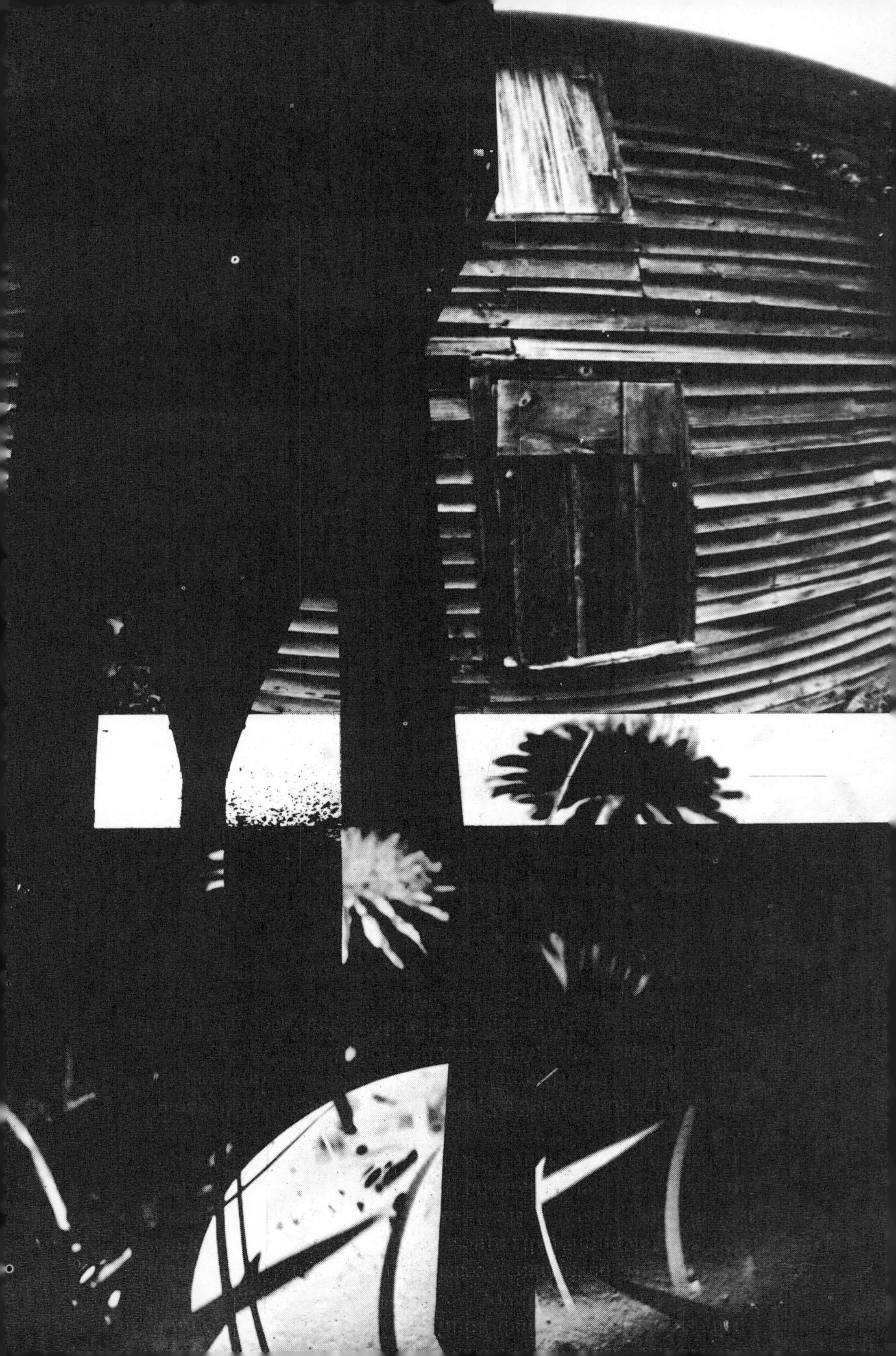

*Dreams are the excursions
to the limbo of things,
a semi-deliverance
from the human prison.*
　AMIEL

Let's consider the 'dreams' which take place on this particular plane of existence—that is, this time and on this planet. There are people who dream about actual people they know (or are familiar with) and see actual events take place.

Days, or weeks, after the dream, they read about the exact event happening to the actual people they were dreaming about. This is called a 'clairvoyant' dream—a dream about an event in the future.

Isn't it possible that the people who have the ability to produce these 'clairvoyant' dreams are actually having an OOBE in which they 'visit' the future and 'see' the events as they occur?

I recall an incident which happened to a close friend who had a vivid clairvoyant dream *but didn't remember it until almost the last moment*. It was an act of *deja vu* (the sensation of realizing that you have experienced something previously—and yet it is taking place now).

He used air travel as casually as you or I use taxis. His business could, with a half hour's notice, take him to London, Berlin or Zurich or Tokyo. He enjoyed flying.

On this particular occasion he was in Chicago and received a telephone call requesting his presence in Los Angeles as soon as possible. He took a cab to O'Hare Airport, purchased a ticket and, as he turned from the ticket window, bumped into a pleasant looking priest and knocked a book from his hand.

My friend apologized profusely as he bent down to pick up the book. Unfortunately the priest also bent down at the same time and their heads knocked together.

It wasn't a severe knock; they both laughed, my friend apologized again and the priest said,

"It's not fatal, my son."

My friend stared at the priest in astonishment because he was certain that he had experienced this incident before. As he watched the priest move rapidly towards the loading gate he knew that someone else was going to bump into the priest. It would be a porter, who turned his head, to say something to someone behind him. As my friend watched—a porter came across the room, carrying a briefcase, turned his head and he bumped into the priest.

Suddenly the entire clairvoyant dream he had experienced the night before, flashed in my friend's mind. He knew exactly what would happen from that moment on.

My friend hurried after the priest, caught up to him and said, "There's no hurry, Father—your flight will be delayed at least twenty minutes. If you would have a cup of coffee with me I'll explain something quite interesting."

The priest looked at my friend carefully, didn't see any signs of madness, and decided to accept the offer.

Over coffee my friend explained the dream he had experienced which began with his bumping into the priest. The plane would blow a tire just as it started down the runway and would be forced to return the passengers to the waiting area.

The priest was skeptical but also amused and, since he was in no hurry, decided to humor my friend and wait to see if the prediction came true. It did. Precisely as my friend had predicted it would. There were no injuries. The passengers were returned to the airport and there was a twenty minute delay.

Neither the priest nor my friend could offer a really satisfactory explanation for the incident.

My friend didn't quite accept my explanation either. While he had to admit that it would be difficult to call it a 'sheer coincidence' he still couldn't bring himself to believe that it was a 'clairvoyant' capability.

You will have the same difficulty until you begin to discover the truth about your dreams. There *is* a way to make that discovery. It has to do with a state of being wherein you are neither 'conscious' nor unconscious.

It is called the hypnoidal area and you enter it before you fall asleep; and you enter it again before you waken. The easiest way for you to recognize the peculiar state is to remind you of an incident that must have happened to you at one time or another.

You must have—at one time or another—been awakened by your alarm clock—reached out, turned it off and then—instead of getting up immediately—decided to stay in bed just for a few minutes.

Now when you made that decision to just lie there for a few minutes—something like this thought occurred to you:

"I really should get up. If I stay here, I'm going to fall asleep and then I'll be late for work."

You know what happened. Exactly what you had predicted.

The next thing you knew—you bolted upright—stared at the clock and groaned. You had overslept and you were going to be late for work.

Do you know why this happened?

You were in an hypnoidal state—and therefore you were in a highly suggestible state. When the thought about oversleeping occurred to you—it was not a thought—but a post-hypnotic suggestion which you had to carry out. In other words, *you* told yourself exactly what you were going to do—and then you did it.

In other words you engaged in auto-hypnosis—self-hypnosis, if you will. That's an extremely important ability that you already possess.

You are going to use that ability to investigate the truth about your dreams. Here's how:

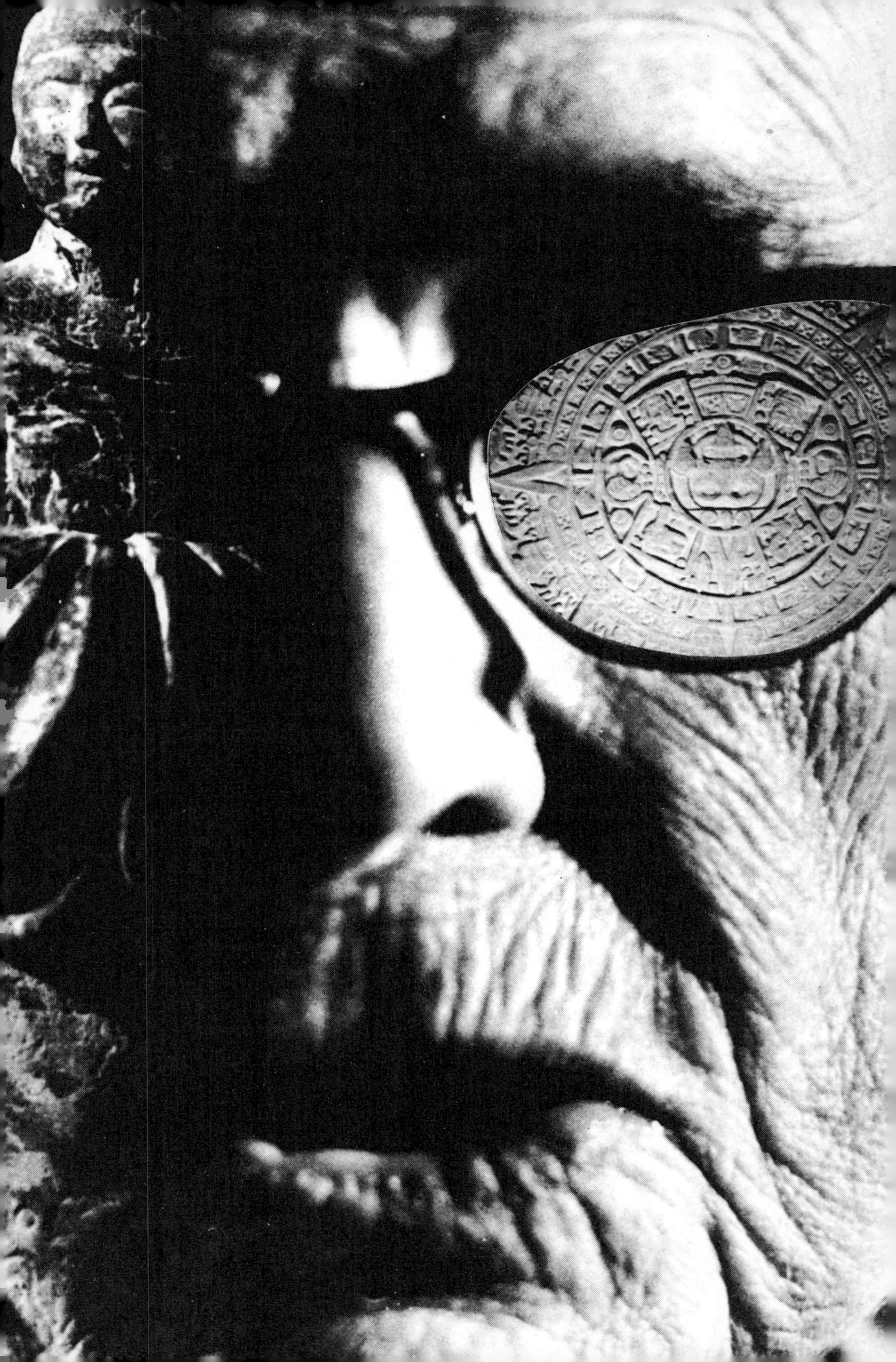

*Vision is the art of
seeing things invisible.*
      SWIFT

Tonight, before you go to bed, you are going to place a large notebook and a black, felt tip pen, on the table or the floor next to your bed.

Then, after you are in bed and just as you feel yourself falling asleep—you will repeat these words in your mind:

I am going to remember every detail of every dream I dream tonight. I will remember every detail or every dream I have tonight. Say that over and over as you fall asleep.

Now—in the morning—before you are fully awake you will say these words: I am going to write down the details of my dreams, clearly and distinctly. I will begin writing on the count of ten. 1-2-3-4-5-6-7-8-9-10.

If you follow those instructions and practice doing this simple auto-hypnosis, every night and morning, you will begin to fill up your notebook with a wide variety of dreams and an astonishing amount of details.

Some of the dreams will be clearly clairvoyant. Others will be obscure, puzzling—possibly distorted or in peculiar time-sequences. For example you may see yourself starting to do something after you have already completed the thing you are just starting.

Don't worry about them, at this point. The meaning will be clear a little later. The point is to practice recording your dreams—and to practice becoming observant in your dreams.

In the majority of cases you know you are dreaming. You are really a spectator in your dreams rather than an active participant—even when it seems you are.

There is a reason for this paradox. It is entirely possible, in your dreams, to be both a spectator and a participant because there are two of you in your dreams.

One of you is trapped in an Earth-bound *conscious* part of your brain (that's the spectator and the reporter); the other part is free of this plane of existence (that's the participant). Your task, as a spectator and reporter is to bring back the details of that *participant's* activities.

As you practice this technique of observing and reporting you will, as you become more skilled in this art, become free of fear and begin to really enjoy these nightly excursions. You will also begin to learn a lot about yourself—and find that you are now capable of a higher awareness during your waking state. You will find that you are more observant and your memory will improve to a point that will astonish people with your ability to demonstrate total recall.

More importantly, later on, you will find that you will be able to answer the many unanswered questions about the true nature of dreams. Finally you will discover the truth in the statement:

You don't have to die to find out what happens after death.

Your next task, now that you have become proficient in the art of observing and reporting your dreams, is to start understanding the true nature of those dreams.

They are all, as you realize now, out-of-body experiences.

Some of them have to do with you—exclusively. They are things that your 'other' self is trying to teach you about yourself. They are messages from your 'higher' intelligence.

Let's examine some of those puzzling and obscure dreams that don't make sense—seem illogical—or out of sequence.

Part of the problem is the fact that these dreams are employing something called 'symbols'—that is objects that represent something other than what they appear to be.

We mentioned the 'censor'—the protective part of the conscious mind that stands guard over certain dreams and tries to prevent them from rising to your conscious mind. Why should there be a 'censor'?

As conscious beings, occupying this particular plane of existence, we are hedged in with all sorts of fears. Most of our repressed feelings revolve around fear.

We are 'afraid' to do certain things because we will be 'punished' if we do. The 'punishment' can range from something as relatively simple as a 'loss of face' or loss of 'standing' in the community—to execution or life imprisonment by the state.

When we are very young and free and uninhibited by fear we discover, in a relatively short time, that the world around us, our parents, siblings, teachers, peer group of children, associates and so forth, have no intention of allowing us to do anything we want to do.

Since our natural inclination is to avoid pain and seek pleasure, the world uses that simple 'either or' to make us conform to rules and regulations governing personal conduct.

If you can think back on your life as a child it would seem to consist of an almost uninterrupted NO! Each time you resisted the no, punishment, in some form or another, resulted. In its simplest form it was pain—swiftly administered.

In the normal course of events you learned quickly how to avoid pain or disapproval and gain pleasure or approval. You usually had to repress something to gain the approval.

Your conscious mind helps you with this repression. It tries to help you eliminate or repress dangerous thoughts.

Repression is a serious business. It requires almost constant pressure. That pressure will cause something else to surface in the form of an aberration or peculiar behavior.

Your higher intelligence wants to eliminate this type of behavior—it wants to tell you why you are doing it. But the 'censor' cannot allow that information to come through *so*—the only way your higher intelligence can get it to you is by disguising the message in 'symbols'.

These 'symbols' are exclusively your symbols. Even though it is true that everyone uses symbols in certain types of dreams they are not universal. They are not interchangeable. There are, it is true certain 'similarities' but they are superficial and not specific. With that thought in mind, let's search for 'symbols' in your dreams.

Pick up your pen, open your notebook to the first distorted dream and read it carefully. Each time you come to an object—a chair, table, door, window, person, staircase, animal, house—any object—underline it.

Go through each obscure, distorted or puzzling dream in the same manner. Underline each object that is mentioned in the dream. Do it carefully and try not to miss any because these are very important.

Long before you have completed this task, certain aspects of each of these dreams will become apparent. You will notice, for example, that some objects are repeated in dream after dream. There are also certain patterns that will be repeated. Combinations of things and actions will also be repeated.

These repeated things, combinations and actions are extremely important because they are, in the main, only variations of the same message.

Your next task will be to transfer all of the underlined words from your notebook to a clean piece of white bond paper—or, if you prefer, a ruled yellow pad.

Here's how. Start with the first dream in which you began to underline objects. You will write down that object name on the clean piece of paper or pad. Keep adding object words, one under the other—unless you come across an object name you have already written. Go back in your list and make a checkmark against that object name. Eventually you will have transferred all of the object names to that clean piece of paper.

Now, close your dream notebook and concentrate on the list you have just completed. Your first concern is with the object name (symbol) that was repeated most often.

Take another piece of clean paper and place that object word (or symbol) at the top of the page. Print it clearly in large capital letters. Look at it. Say it aloud. Now try to think of as many words as you can that are similar to that object rod printed at the top of the page.

Write down all the words you can think of.

Now try to find words that sound like that object word. It doesn't matter if the sound isn't exactly the same.

The idea is not to inhibit yourself. Say the same sounding words aloud. As you find each similar sounding word—write it down directly underneath the object-name. When you have exhausted all possibilities try a different approach.

Start thinking of words that are the opposite in meaning to the object-name printed at the top of the page. Or if you can't think of direct opposites think of opposites in terms of function—what the object is for.

Say each word you find—aloud—then write it down in a new group of words directly under the first group. Again—when you have examined all possibilities—try another approach.

This time try to find humor in the word. Try a playful approach such as a 'pun' on the word. You might also try to think of the object-name in terms of a joke. Is there any joke that you can think of that might use that object-name in a funny or humorous way? Write it down.

You should, by now, have three distinct groups of words of descriptions of the object-name on that piece of paper.

Yes—I know it's not easy—but it's important because you are training yourself to 'see' things differently.

We are now going to re-check that list. Start with the first group. Has anything else occurred to you? Have you thought of an additional word in this category? Write it down in that group. Do the same with the next group of words. Any omissions? Write them down. Finally, your third and last group should be re-read. Are there any puns—any play on words—any jokes that you have overlooked. Write them down.

Open your dream notebook again. Begin reading the first dream in which this particular object-name was mentioned. Read the dream all the way through. Then read the next one, paying attention to where and under what circumstances that object-name was mentioned. Read each one of your dreams until you have completed the dozen dreams.

Something—by this time—must have suggested itself to you during this re-examination of your dreams. There must have been some kind of pattern—some kind of a combination that became apparent with re-reading.

However—if you have not yet found it—and the deeper meaning attached to that object-name is not yet clear—don't worry about it—your computer is working on it.

Now let's start to investigate the content of your dream.

First we must remember that what your dream is in actuality is a 'symbolic' message from you—to you. It's actually a message from part of *you* in another dimension.

What we are going to do is search for symbols.

Pick up your ballpoint pen—open your notebook to your first recorded dream and read it carefully. Each time you come to an object in your dream—a chair, table, door, window, staircase, house, animal, person—anything, underline that object with your pen.

Go through each of your dreams in sequence underlining objects as you do so. Do this carefully. Try not to miss any. If you have a doubt as to whether or not it's an object underline it anyway—we can always eliminate it later.

Just remember that each part of that dream—of all your dream was deliberately created by you; not the conscious you—the other aspect of you that's called the sub-conscious. However it's still you and since you created each of your dreams you really know what the deeper meaning is.

As you continue to work at it you may find that the real meaning will flash in your mind like a sudden explosion of recognition. Or perhaps it will flash through your mind so quickly that it will be gone before you can grasp it.

Even if that does happen—take heart—because it means that you're getting close to the truth and if you persist you will suddenly find the meaning.

Above all—be courageous. If the meaning should appear to be repugnant or even disgusting to you—do not shy away from it. Face it. Accept it. That acceptance will be followed by a strong sensation of relief.

That relief is the surest sign that you have found the true meaning hidden in your dream. It's a guarantee that you have discovered the truth.

Continue your investigation of the next most frequently used object-name. List it in bold capital letters at the top of another letter-sized piece of paper.

Keep in mind, at all times, that there is a special meaning to you in that object-name. Remember that it's being used as a symbol of something.

Go through the same procedure with this *second* object-name as you did with the first one. Say the word aloud. Ring changes on the word. Try the opposites. Try to find humor in it. And remember to write down each word that occurs to you in each of the three groups of words.

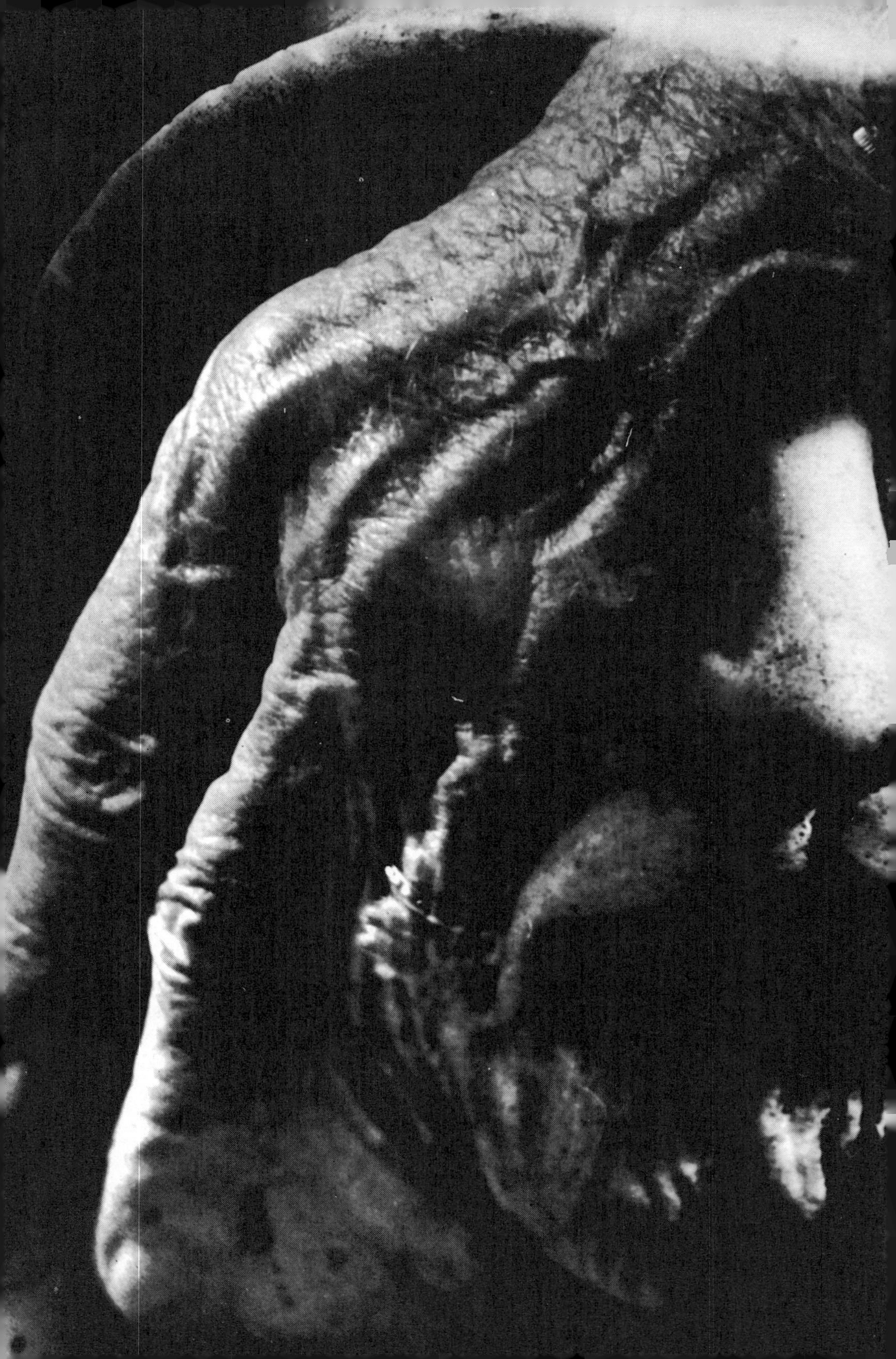

*This is
the stuff
that dreams
are made of.*
   SHAKESPEARE

Now open your dream notebook again and begin to read each of your dreams keeping the second object-name in the forefront of your mind.

Try to form an opinion, at this point of the tone of the dream. Was it a happy one—unhappy—funny—pleasant—unpleasant—frightening—inspiring—depressing?

Was it vivid or vague? What about color?

Did you recognize anyone in the dream? A friend—relative—enemy—public figure—movie or TV star?

How were they dressed? How were *you* dressed? Were you undressed—partially dressed?

These are some of the 'clues' we mentioned earlier. Each of them can help you towards understanding the hidden message the dream contains.

Can you remember whether the dream took place in the daytime—night time—a particular season?

Close your notebook—put away your lists for a few moments while we discuss some other aspects of your dreams that may help you when you return to your work.

Let's talk about your dreams from the standpoint of the you that keeps producing these dreams each night. It is not the conscious part of your mind that's doing this.

Yes—I know that you 'day-dream' but that's entirely different. When you do that you are indulging in fantasy. Fantasy is a different kind of activity because there is no use of symbols in a fantasy. You deal with actual persons and objects in their usual relationship to the objective world. Your fantasy deals with imagined activities in which you play a desired role.

In a sexual fantasy you usually play a different role than the one you generally play in real life. In a real or imagined situation—such as a re-play of an actual scene that might have happened in your office you recast yourself in the winning role.

Fantasy is a harmless activity that is quite simple to understand and analyze because it is directly presented.

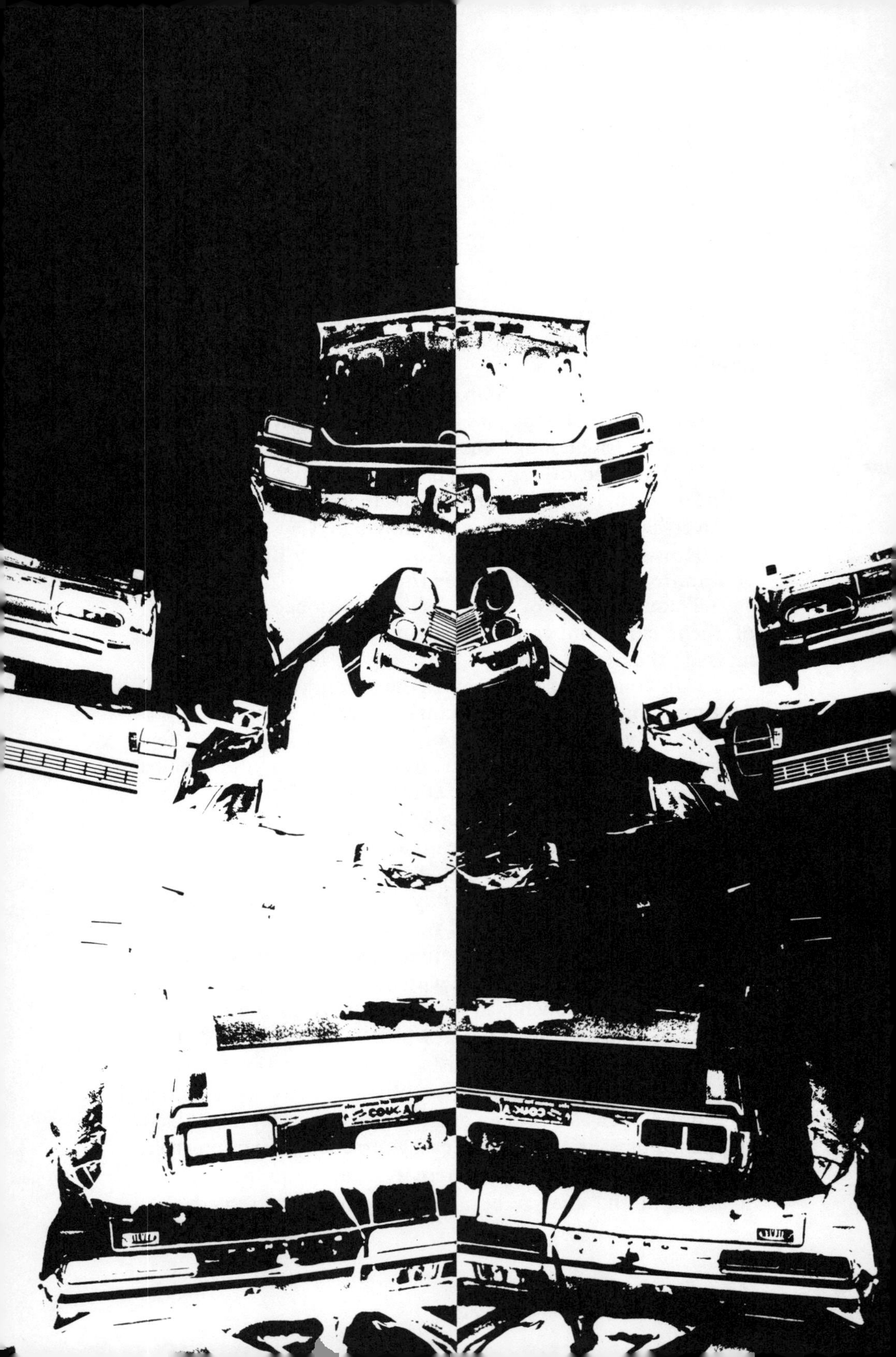

*Superfluous wealth
can buy superfluities only.*
       THOREAU

Dreams are indirectly presented and are filled with *symbols*. Dreams deal with a different kind of reality. They also deal with a different kind of dimension because they are produced by a dimensionally different you.

This different you inhabits a different world than you do and because it does it *thinks* differently than you do. However it is entirely sympathetic towards you and does try to provide clues so that you may recognize what it's trying to tell you.

You will discover, as you progress in your ability to analyze your own dreams, that the clues are, in many cases, so obvious that you will have to laugh at yourself for failing to see them immediately. The reason for this is that they are so simple—so obvious—that you cannot accept them.

"It can't be that simple!" is your first natural reaction.

Oh, yes it can. In many cases—particularly with fleeting dreams—it really is that simple. Let me show you with an example of something that happened to me.

When I was a schoolboy, in my teens, I began to have a recurring dream that frightened me. It was a simple—fleeting type of dream—in which I would find myself in a doctor's office, because I had this severe pain at the base of my skull.

The odd part was—that each time I awoke there was no pain at all. I was puzzled but not really frightened until the night that the doctor looked at me with a frown and shook his head. "This has to be removed," he said solemnly.

I was really frightened because now I was convinced that the dream was a warning that something was seriously wrong. I decided to go to our family doctor after school and get a complete physical checkup.

He was surprised but delighted at my maturity in making a decision to have a physical checkup. Naturally I never mentioned the dream or my fear.

I was relieved to hear that I was disgustingly healthy.

When I came home, my mother told me that my aunt, who had been staying with us for the past two weeks, had decided to go home. The first thought that popped into my head at this news was,

"I'm so glad that *pain in the neck* has gone!"

Like a flash I realized the meaning behind my dream and knew that I'd never dream it again. I didn't like my aunt and I hated the idea of her staying at our house. I think I was afraid that she would stay indefinitely. She was a real pain in the neck!

So you see—your dream can be quite simple at times as well as highly complex and involved. If you seek and unravel the *simple* dreams it will give you confidence and make it much easier for you to unravel the complex dreams.

Now, perhaps, you can understand why I asked you to consider puns and play on words when you were listing your object-name comparisons.

Sometimes a cliche or proverb may be the clue. There have been cases where nursery rhymes were used. Advertising slogans might be the clue. The type of clue used is—in many cases—designed to 'fit' your particular hobbies—your profession—your work—something that is familiar to you.

Don't dismiss the simple dream as unimportant. There are times when your analysis of a simple dream can have a dramatic effect on your daily life. It might offer you the solution to the reason why you are unhappy or depressed or uneasy. The relief that comes with the understanding the simple dream provides, is important to your general well being. Don't ignore the simple dream in favor of the complex ones.

Of course the big, fat, complex dreams are fascinating. They can also be very frightening too. Particularly when they are recurring dreams. Some people—who are easily frightened or highly suggestible—will become afraid to sleep because they dread facing the nightmare they know is waiting for them as soon as they fall asleep.

You must have heard reference, at one time or another, to the term 'sexual symbols' with reference to dream symbols. Here again we find that there is a false premise at work. That will become evident if you think about it.

For example—the phallic symbol—which, according to the 'authorities' is any object that resembles a penis. Conversely, any object that contains a crevice, aperture, depression, or what have you, is considered to be a female sexual symbol—the vagina.

Now let's employ some basic logic. There are only four basic closed shapes namely: circle, square, triangle and star. All other shapes are variants of this group.

Now if we consider each one in turn, starting with the circle, we find: a circle would be considered as a female sexual symbol. However, if we elongated that circle and made it into an elipse we would have a male sexual symbol. The same goes for each shape. If we saw a square (box) we automatically have a vagina—but if we elongated it into a narrow rectangle we then have a phallic symbol. A triangle, with the point down, is obviously the pubic area (female) but a triangle on its side with a narrow base and long sides is phallic.

The point that I am trying to make is that *any* object could be considered as a sexual symbol but that does not mean that it is automatically.

With all due deference to Dr. Freud everything in this world does not revolve around sex. Everyone in this world is not bothered with sexual problems exclusively. There are quite a few people who have satisfactory sex lives. There are many people who are not repressed—not concerned with whether they are normal.

These people dream every night of their life.

Should they consider every object they see in their dreams as having sexual connotations? Of course not. If you *are* having difficulty with your sex life then there is a strong possibility that many of your symbols are sexually oriented. A possibility—*not* a certainty.

What I want you to remember is this: do not prejudge your symbols. Try to examine them objectively from many different standpoints otherwise you will fall into the habit of immediately assuming that they are sex symbols. That would make it very difficult for you to gain true insight into the *truth* of the message in your dreams.

Not all dreams are necessarily sexually oriented.

As you continue with your efforts to gain skill in the recording as well as the interpretation of your 'dreams' you will begin to see that there is much more to it than merely 'dreaming'. You will begin to 'see' the other reality that exists in that 'other' higher plane of existence. You will begin to see what the Early Stone Age Man 'saw' and tried to imitate with his ritual magic and his labyrinths.

You will begin to understand that your 'dreams' are real and not imaginary. That the act of dreaming is, in reality, a bridge that enables you to penetrate that 'other' world that exists just beyond the perimeter of this one.

With that understanding in mind you can begin to unravel the mystery of mysteries—the truth of 'where you go' and 'what happens' after you die. You will no longer be afraid of the unknown because you begin to realize that there is no 'unknown' at all. There is only reality—total reality and death is only a portion of that reality. It is not the end of reality only a phase—a necessary passage between lives.

*We that acquaint ourselves with every zone
and pass both tropics and behold the poles
When we come home are to ourselves unknown
and unacquainted still with our own souls.*

JOHN DAVIES—Nosce Teipsum 1599

chapter 10

achievement of self

The great civilizations of the past did not come into being overnight. Even with the new powers he enjoyed, thanks to his 'altered' brain, Man did not create the powerful city-states in a matter of years or centuries.

It took approximately seven thousand years for Man to move out of the forests and caves; to initate and develop the arts of sowing and harvesting; to acquire the skills involved in transforming the milk of goats and cows into butter and cheeses; to learn and perfect the art of weaving material.

In Egypt, for example—as well as in Mesopotamia—the wealth and growth of the future empires of Egypt, Babylonia and Assyria, were dependent upon Man's ability to tame the rivers—the Nile in Egypt and the Tigris and Euphrates in Mesopotamia.

This meant centuries of experimentation with different systems of flood control; with dikes; with the problems of drainage and the harvesting of flood water.

During this long period, new concepts came into being— language and writing—and a new aristocracy of *knowledge*.

Knowledge gained and transmitted meant *power*. Power, for some men, became the most desired thing and they sought it—gained it—fought to keep and control it.

One aspect of this system was most interesting. Before a man could become an artisan or a tradesman, he first had to serve in the temple under the tutorship of the priests.

Only such knowledge as he needed to become fairly proficient at his chosen profession was transmitted to him— together with the catechisms necessary for the perpetuation of the state-religion.

This sort of knowledge/power/conservation was the key to the rise of the great city-states—the great empires of the newly 'civilized' world.

In one variation or another, this 'concept' remained almost intact, throughout the world, until the advent of the

American Revolution, which was followed by the French Revolution, and the kingdoms began to topple.

Knowledge gained and transmitted is *power*. That power, thanks to the advent of the printing press, passed to the great mass of the people, it was no longer the tool of the 'aristocracy'.

The power of the 'gods' had vanished, too. The half animal-half Man god had faded into obscurity, left to gaze blankly from the dusty niches of ruined temples in Egypt, Mesopotamia and Mexico.

A new god had been created called 'science' and the priests of this new religion were called 'scientists'. This new breed of Man created a new 'language of science'.

Only those who served an apprenticeship in the temples of 'science' were permitted to learn and use this new language and so that all man should know them they were given special insignia called 'degrees' which were displayed conspicuously.

This new priesthood then began to exercise the power of the new and secret knowledge. They began to create a new and different world—a world filled with new 'concepts'.

We shall speak of two of these disciples of science.

Sir Isaac Newton, the mathematical genius, was born in the middle of the 17th Century (1642) and died in the first quarter of the 18th Century (1727).

He was a full professor at the age of 27 and during the 85 years of his full and active life he made many extremely valuable contributions to the world of science.

Newton was the first to show the usefulness of the binomial theorem; invented differential calculus and integral calculus; was first to conceive the concept of universal gravitation; was responsible for a new theory of light and color and originated the concept of the corpuscular emission of light (as opposed to the wave theory of light transmission).

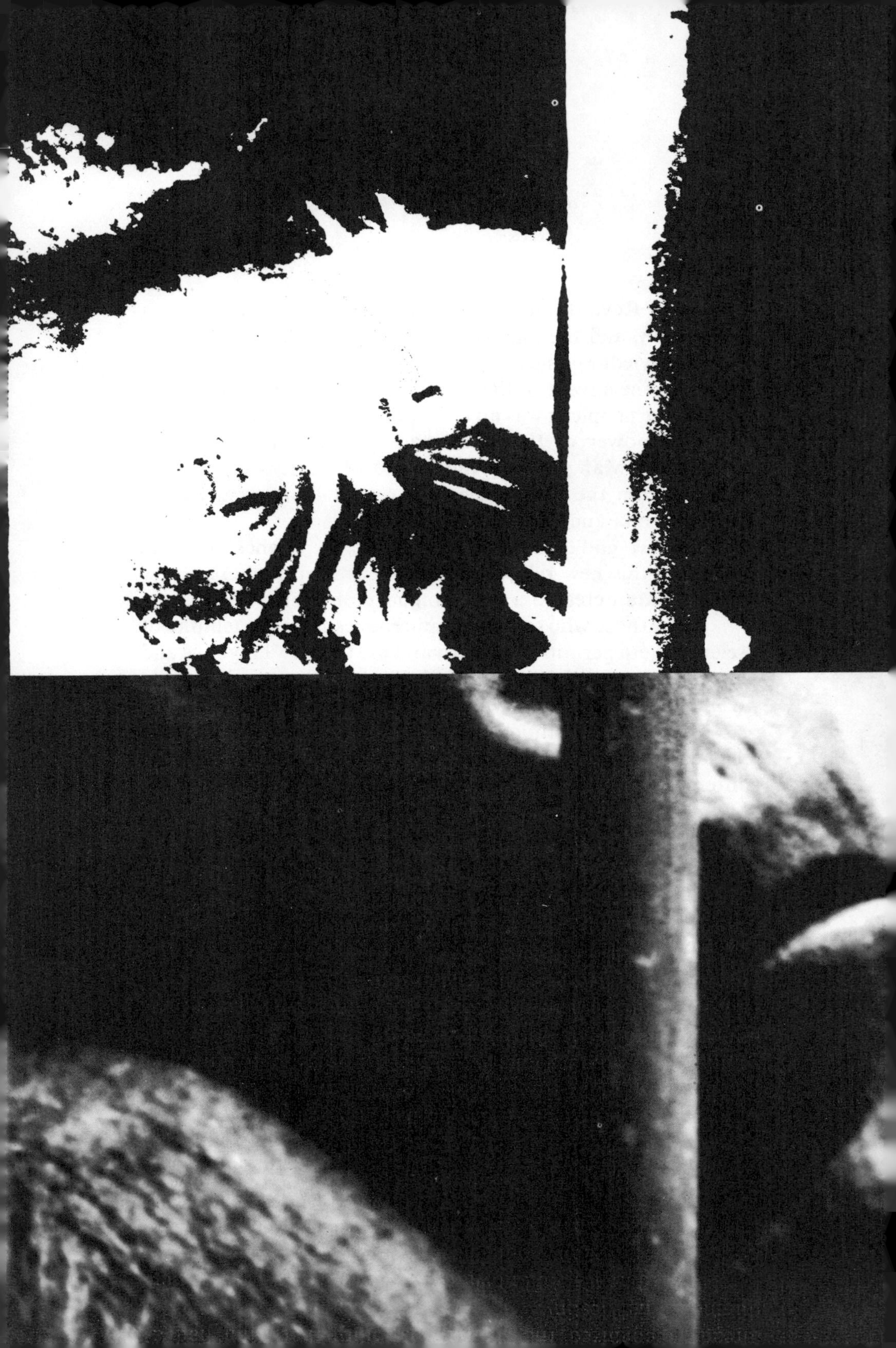

Man is God's ape, and an ape is zany to man, doing over those tricks (especially if they be knavish) which he sees done before him.
          DEKKER

Newton was a remarkable example of *Homo Sapiens Sapiens* who, almost single-handedly laid the foundation for the science of physics.

Albert Einstein, the mathematical genius, was born in the first quarter of the 19th Century and died in the middle of the 20th Century (1955).

Einstein published his astonishing theory of relativity at the age of 26. Subsequently, he published his remarkable unified field theory which includes, in a single mathematical formula, the laws of electromagnetism and gravitation. He explained and gave the formula for Brownian movement; was the first to deduce the influence of gravity on the propogation of light and developed the law of photoelectric effect to explain the transformation of light quanta.

His most important contribution was to demonstrate that Newtonion physics was only valid on *Earth* and that once Man moved beyond the terrestrial to the extra-terrestrial an entirely new kind of physics was needed.

Einstein, just a few years after the turn of the century, had already recognized the strong possibility that Man had a diminensional destiny.

He had no way of knowing that in less than a decade after he'd departed, Man would have the ability to hurl himself through space in complete defiance of gravitational force.

Our altered ape has moved with dazzling speed.

In a twinkling of an eye he has moved from the art of making primitive stone tools to the art of fashioning sophisticated thunderbolts with which he proposes to tame the universe beyond his door.

And still, with all his vaunted technology, Man has barely moved an inch towards his true destiny.

The ape is still there.

> "...but man, proud man, drest in a little brief authority, most ignorant of what he's most assured, his glassy essence, like an angry ape, plays such fantastic tricks before high heaven, as make the angels weep."

William Shakespeare made that keen observation in his play "Measure For Measure" in 1604.

It might have been written yesterday.

The evidence of the ape's activities surrounds us on all sides; screams at us from the headlines of the newspapers; assails our ears via radio and television newscasts; stalks us in the darkened streets; in the supermarket parking lots; in the hallways of our apartment house.

The ape is still here.

We can only marvel at the patience of our 'visitors' from outer space and wonder what they must feel as they witness what the ape is doing with the miraculous gift they gave him.

They are keeping tabs on their creation. In much the same manner as a scientist will return to observe his guinea pigs from time to time.

They are not dismayed because they were well aware of the consequences. If anything they are well pleased that a few specimens have achieved the destiny planned for them. They are confident that, given sufficient time, more will follow.

We are all aware of the 'few' who have achieved what they were meant to achieve from the very beginning.

Patterns in the mind of Man.

Images that cannot be altered, erased or, in the end, prevented from emerging with blinding clarity.

A portal—a doorway—in the mind, which the 'few' have opened and entered into the reality of being.

The list of the 'few' who have achieved their dimensional destiny is clearly written; it blazes with eternal light against the darkness of the deeds of the 'angry ape' down the centuries.

Philosophers, teachers, prophets, the noblest minds of all time—the handful that 'saw' what was hidden and tried to show us the path we had to follow and were—in the main—ignored, scorned, maimed, mutilated and murdered.

There is no need to 'name' the few—their works are with us—*that* cannot be obliterated nor can the uneasy feeling that they were *right*.

When Hamlet said, "*There are more things in heaven and earth, Horatio, than are dreamt of in your philosophy.*" ... he spoke a profound truth.

Shakespeare saw truth plainly, clearly, without reservation. As did Gautama, the Buddha—as did Jesus of Nazareth—as did Paul—as did *all* the 'few'.

And the truth shall set you free.

The truth is within you—the ape cannot touch it.

Let's employ some simple logic, for the moment. Do you suppose that our 'visitors' with their super-intelligence and their immense ability to see into eons of time as easily as we can see across the street—do you suppose, for one moment, that they engaged in this difficult experiment for no reason?

Of course there was a reason. They—the visitors are fulfilling their destiny as surely as we must fulfill our destiny. They are simply the 'tools' of an even *greater* intelligence.

Let's take the matter of *dimensions*.

Do you recall, in earlier chapter—Chapter Five—The Visible and Invisible World—when I asked you to perform a simple experiment in dimensions?

Do you remember your sensation of being a 'god' to the little two-dimensional creatures who inhabited their limited two-dimensional world?

Our visitors from outer space are 'gods' to you because they operate in your three-dimensional world with their extra-dimensional capabilities, as easily as you operated in that two-dimensional world.

The difference is that you also have the capability of entering their world—and the worlds beyond that.

You may enter those worlds through the portal in your brain—implanted there almost 100,000 years ago.

The strange part is that you know that it's there.

You've always known it. As a very young child you used that portal frequently. You did it as easily as you breathed.

Because you were innocent.

You still use the portal each night of your life. Each time you dream you enter another dimension. And you dream a lot—much more than you could possibly imagine. In fact, it has been proven that if you are continually prevented from dreaming over a long period of time—say three or four nights running—you become disoriented—languish and eventually will die.

Your dream life is a necessity—not a luxury.

If you have ever wondered at the insistence of analysts, psycho-therapists and the lot, upon your making an effort to remember and recount your dreams... the answer is that the truth lies in them.

And the truth shall set you free.

The truth in your dreams is not only a dimensional truth but, more importantly, it is the truth about *you* and your deepest feelings, desires, frustrations and—your destiny.

The innocent are free—free to move in any dimension but with the loss of innocence there is a corresponding loss of freedom to escape the confines of this dimension.

Can innocence, once lost, be regained?

No—but you shouldn't want to regain it. To regain it you would have to revert to a primitive state of being.

Your task is to move upwards, to a higher plane of being, to a higher dimension.

There is only one way to do that. It's the most incredibly difficult way—but the only way, and that's through complete acceptance of the truth.

You know the truth—the absolute, unvarnished truth about yourself. No other human knows it. Only you. And your terrible task is to admit it—freely, without reservation.

To do that you must do another extremely difficult thing. You must forgive yourself. I mean that in the literal sense. For it is you, and you alone, who have judged and condemned you.

So long as that judgment and condemnation stands, so long shall you be blind to the truth. So long shall you stand, frustrated and unhappy, unable to pass through the portal in your brain.

You are the final court of appeals. You, and you alone can reverse the decision that has been made against you. You, and you alone can forgive and pardon.

You are not an animal.

Unless you want to be an animal. That's the easiest thing in the world to do.

You are not an angry ape.

Unless you want to be an angry ape. That, too, is an easy achievement. Anyone can do it. The majority of people do it.
The apes are all over the land as thick as the sands of the sea—if I may paraphrase Ibsen.

The apes sit in high places as well as low.

When someone says to you,
"When you die, you're dead and that's it. Don't be a sucker. Take everything you can get and the hell with the other guy. Just look out for number one. Don't believe all that crap about your immortal soul—it's just hogwash. It's just a way they use to keep you in line."

That's an ape speaking.

He happens to be telling the truth—as far as *he* is concerned because when an ape dies that is the end of it. His idea about the immortal soul is correct. He doesn't have one.
You must understand one thing quite clearly. Our 'visitors' from outer space only altered the brain of Homo Erectus—they did not give him a soul.
The pattern of images they implanted in that altered brain only gave Man the opportunity to fully realize his potential.

An immortal soul is something that you have to reach out for—it's not a gift that can be handed out like a pass to a movie.
Now, perhaps, you can understand the *truth* that underlines some of the statements that apes make.

> "All that crap about the Devil and wanting your immortal soul. You got any idea how many times I said—Okay! Let's make a deal. You can have my soul and this is what I want for it!—and nothing—but nothing happened. So you see? All that stuff about the Devil and your soul is pure crap."

The ape who made that statement didn't realize that he had nothing to bargain with. He didn't have a soul in the first place so his offer was meaningless.

Can you imagine anyone, with the full knowledge of the meaning of an immortal soul, who would be willing to barter it away for anything that Earth had to offer?

Only an ignorant ape would be capable of such crass thinking. Only an ape would have the temerity to believe that his existence justified his receipt of a soul.

The apes of this world will dissolve into nothing because that's what they are—nothing. They were formed from nothing—strove to *achieve* nothing—and succeeded in becoming nothing.

They have swaggered down the halls of Time; lied, cheated, raped and murdered their way to power and now, triumphant upon their dungheap of illusion, have only the blackness of inevitable nothingness to look forward to. It's a just reward.

> Tomorrow, and tomorrow, and tomorrow
> Creeps in this petty pace from day to day
> To the last syllable of recorded time;
> And all our yesterdays have lighted fools
> The way to dusty death. Out, out brief candle!
> Life's but a walking shadow, a poor player
> That struts and frets his hour upon the stage
> And then is heard no more; it is a tale
> Told by an idiot, full of sound and fury
> Signifying nothing.
>
> Shakespeare's MACBETH.

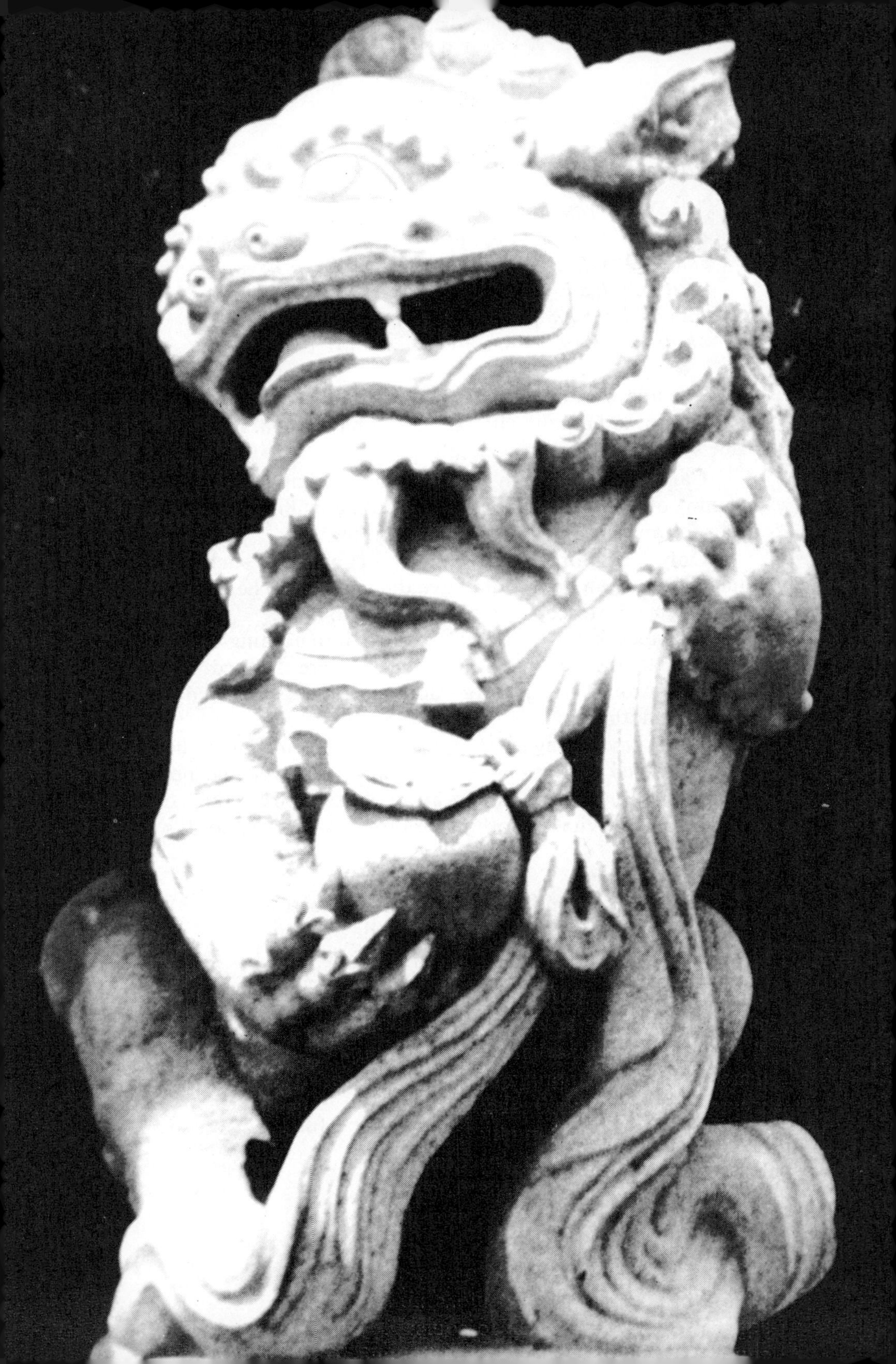

The gods are not sorcerers who change themselves from time to time, nor are they misled by the machinations of others in either word or deed.
                    PLATO

We have come a long way, you and I, on this voyage that began in the swirling mists of Earth's beginnings. Now, as we stand, in essence, upon this towering point in Time, we can look back and see, stretched before us like a fantastic mural, your inexorable progress from the darkness of the primeval forests into the brilliant, eternally lighted vastness of Space.

Yes—it was your journey—your progress—your determination that has led you to this particular launching platform which, in a short time, will hurl you to the distant galaxies.

You are the same *Homo Sapiens Sapiens* who stood, dazzled with the sudden realization that you could 'see' much more than just the world around you—thanks to the 'altered' brain you had been given.

100,000 years have vanished in the twinkling of an eye. All that is past is just prologue. You have not even begun to reach your greatest achievements.

Everything that has gone before was a product of your childhood—you are just now beginning to reach into your adulthood. The best is yet to come.

You are beginning to move now—with ever increasing speed—towards the destiny you were created for back in that dank and mysterious forest.

You are beginning to reach an understanding of what you really are. You know now that you are not an animal; that you never *were* an animal; but rather that you are a singular creation—a rare and unique being, the only conceived and created entity on this planet since it was formed out of that incredible mass of boiling gas many billions of years ago.

You know now that you are the only creature on Earth capable of dealing in symbols—symbols that you have spent considerable time with during the past 100,000 years—and will spend an even long period of time within the eons to come.

It is this extraordinary ability to synthesize existence to transform experience as well as the gaps in experience into easily handled symbolic concepts that not only makes you unique but insures that you will achieve your destiny.

Let us consider exactly what the reasons were behind your creation and why you were made the way you are.

Your creators—the 'gods' from outer space—most certainly designed your structure to resemble them as closely as possible. There are some differences due to the differences in the world they came from but, in the main, there is an easily recognized similarity.

How do we know this? Simply because it's one of the oldest memories in your mind. You have repeated this theme endlessly—on the walls of caves—in your ages of carving and sculpting—in your writings—from the very beginning.

You were created in the image of your maker.

Yes—you were created. You did not evolve from any one-celled entity. The primate structure was selected because it is the ideal structure. They wanted you to be a biped, with freedom to use your hands. They made very few changes in the physiological apparatus—only in the elongation of the skeleton—the enlargement of your skull so that it would accept the double-sized brain.

Then you were programmed—just like a computer—given certain basics—and a unique synaptic switchboard which would permit you to 'visualize' the unseeable.

Then they stepped back and let you start off on your own with full confidence that you would eventually find your way to your true destiny.

You were off and running in a flash. Your obviously superior mentality—your ability to 'see' what animals could not—your remarkable ability to grasp concepts—to create symbols which eventually became language—not only helped you to survive in the incredibly hostile world you found yourself in—it enabled you to conquer the physical world in a relatively short time.

Yet—all the while you were satisfying your continuous physiological needs—there was another hunger gnawing at your brain. It was a puzzle that had to be solved.

You knew, instinctively, that the solution to the puzzle lay in a thing called truth. Your task was to uncover this truth—to 'see' it in your mind—to ultimately know the totality of that eternal and absolute truth that was waiting for you somewhere in the vast universe.

You began with an attempt to form a philosophy—a way of investigating the anatomy of reality and its relation to your being and ultimate purpose.

It was a truly formidable undertaking—even with your remarkable 'altered' brain and extraordinary capability.

Remember—in the beginning there was nothing to guide you—no language—no books—no previous experience to rely upon—nothing. *Just a continuous need to know.*

It took a considerable amount of patience to continue, in the face of endless failure—disappointments—defeats and frustrations—but you persisted.

One unending source sustained you through all of the trials—all of the seemingly endless years. Your dreams. That precious stuff—that stream of messages which flowed steadily through your mind as you slept. This was the staff that supported you—encouraged you to continue your seemingly hopeless quest for the truth.

Then language came—and what a marvellous boon that was—because now you could join with other minds—with other thinkers and compare—restructure—reorganize and build even sounder foundations.

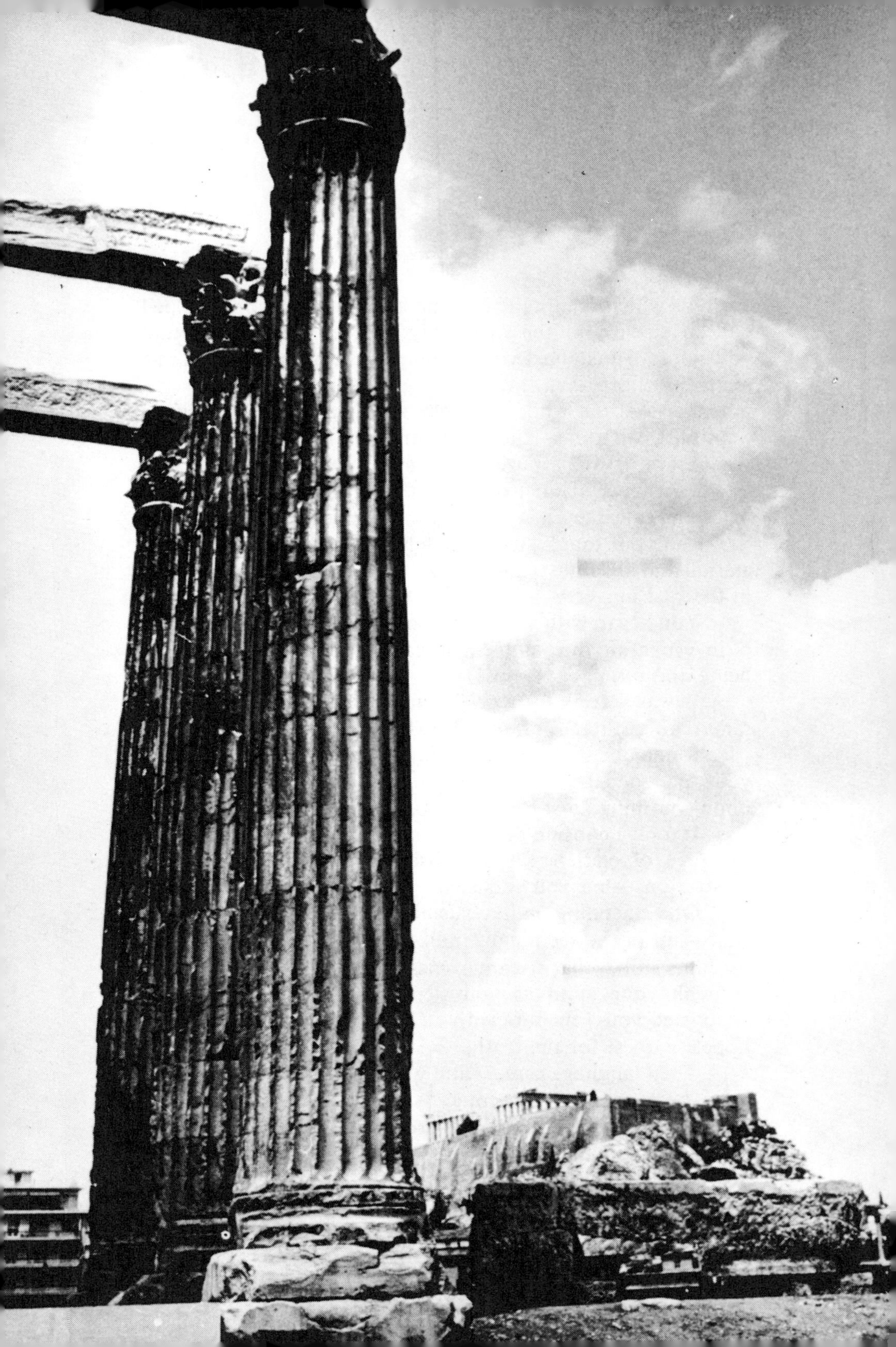

The truth in religion lies in its very obscurity and in the little light we have on it, and in our indifference to that light.
       PASCAL

Then—an even greater gift arrived—*writing*. Now you began to conquer Time itself. Your *thought* could be captured—imprisoned—be made into a legacy for yourself in future years. Now you could penetrate Time—could be free of Time—could outwit inexorable Time.

Now you began to build a tower of Thought. You built a structure into which you could pour the fruit of your labors—the stuff which would eventually permit you to unlock the door to the ultimate mystery.

Now, in quick succession, you created logic, ethics, aesthetics, metaphysics. Each was like a torch that lighted a new corner in the darkness. With each new creation the light became brighter, the darkness was receding more and more.

This new light gave life to new thoughts, new ideas, new concepts which permitted you to re-examine the myths and legends—your previous creations—with fresh new insight as to their validity.

A new horizon appeared. You could feel a tingling in your mind—you were certain that truth, like the sun, would surely appear shortly on that horizon.

It didn't happen. Somehow that horizon, like the deceptive mountain, was much further away than it appeared to be. As you approached it—somehow it moved further away.

You were puzzled by this. You had been so sure—so certain—that the truth would rise. But it didn't.

So now you decided to try something entirely different.

You came into being (again, as you had so many times in the past) in 470 B.C. in Athens that great city-state of Greece.

Your father, Sophroniscus—and your mother Pharanete—were well-to-do, upperclass people of better than average intelligence and education. Your father's friendship with Aristedes denotes the status of your family in society.

Your name was Socrates and—after an excellent education and a rather distinguished political career, you were ready to create the body of work which was to mark you above all men till the end of time.

Your timing was perfect. You had arrived at that point in the Age of Pericles when it was quite evident that the 'science' of that age was on the verge of bankruptcy. An exciting century, which had started in the 5th Century, was ending in the 6th Century with a mass of contradictory 'schools of thought' relative to the nature of the Earth and the 'cosmos'—which is the Greek concept of the opposite of chaos.

Thinking men throughout Greece were abandoning science because it was hopelessly mired in fallacious reasoning and stubborn negativism.

It was time—high time—for a new and different approach to the age old problems. Your approach was different—so different that it generated a new Age of Thought with an excitingly fresh viewpoint that would have far reaching effects on the generation of thinkers to come after you.

You proposed the unique idea that Man was a 'soul' that *used* a body. You further stated that it was the 'nature' of that soul which was the root of Man's happiness or unhappiness.

It was quite obvious that no man wanted unhappiness. Yet he was unhappy—even with wealth, health, fame, strength, success—everything. Why was that?

The reason was simple. You stated that, happiness or unhappiness is dependent upon the nature of the 'soul'. If the soul was good—then happiness resulted. If the soul was bad then unhappiness would result.

The first and fundamental recipe for happiness was that Man should know good and then he would not be capable of willing anything else *but* good.

All virtue, you said, resides in the knowledge of good.

All vice is the ignorance of true good.

Popular notions of goodness—that which passes for virtue—is an illusion. Popular goodness is the kind of habit that breaks easily under temptation.

The knowledge of good is the only kind of knowledge in the world that cannot be ill-used. Possession of the knowledge of good guarantees that it will only be used in a proper manner.

These are exciting concepts but your fame does not rest upon them but rather upon a method of teaching—a method of stimulating thought in the minds of pupils.

Your method, naturally called the 'Socratic Method' is the simple, but highly effective method of *questioning* evolved from the thought that it was not 'facts' which were suspect—but the statements people *made* with regard to those facts.

You demonstrated that by questioning you could make a person consider the consequences which must result if a statement or hypothesis is carried to a conclusion.

There is little doubt that you made a great contribution, not only to your own society, but the generations of 'truth seekers' who would follow you and your teachings.

Unfortunately, your fame as well as your adherence to the principals of 'goodness' which you formulated, led to your arrest and condemnation to death by hemlock. You were offered an opportunity to escape but naturally repudiated it because it would have negated everything you stood for and espoused. So you took the hemlock and died at the age of 70, still in your prime mentality.

Your next appearance—as Aristotle—gave further impetus to thought and a new Age of Reason appeared on the horizon—there was new hope that the end of the quest was in sight. Order and reason; logic and rhetoric the advent of the syllogism—all the stuff necessary to fire the furnaces of thought and bring a swift and very satisfactory conclusion to the long and arduous journey.

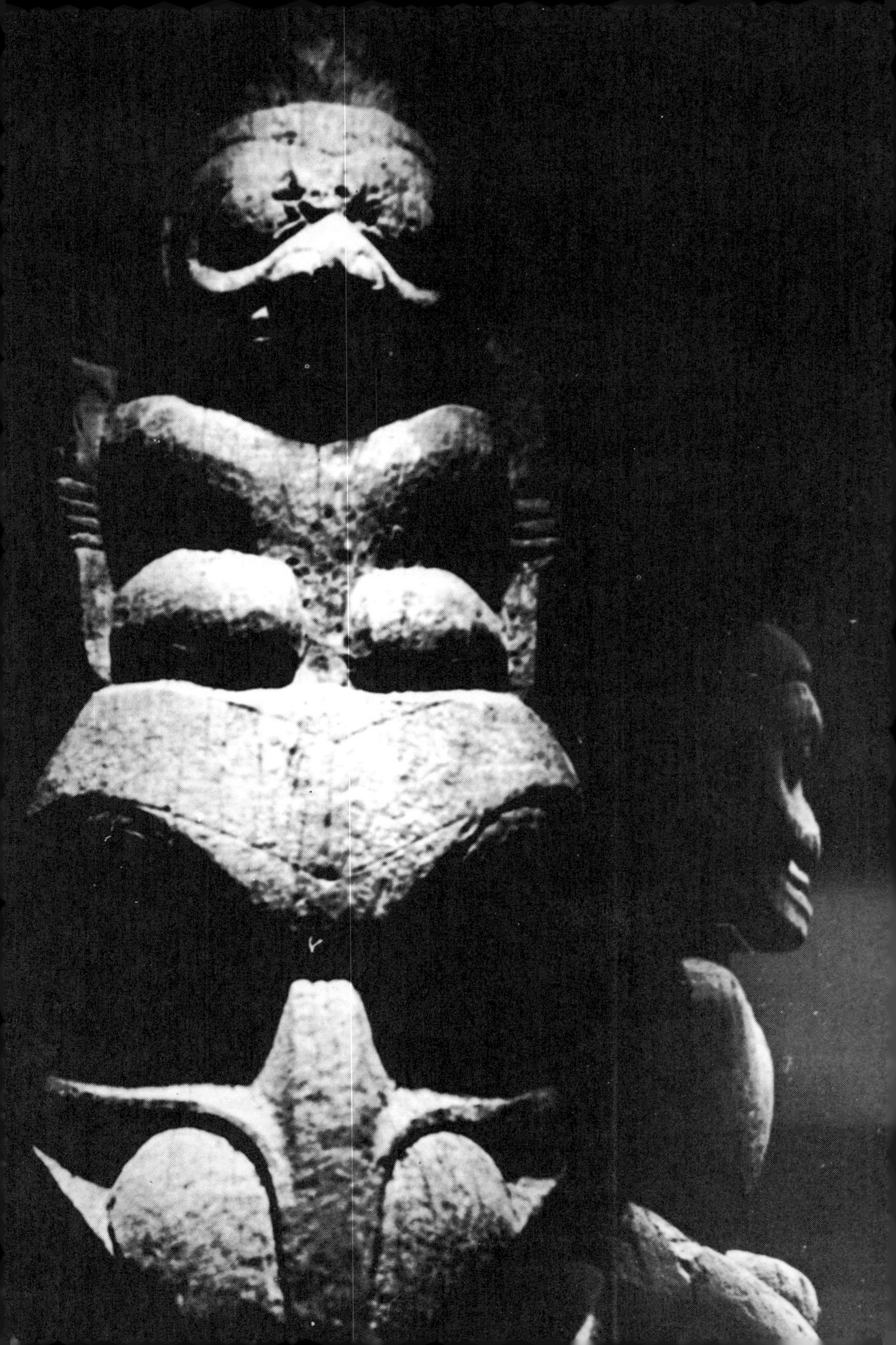

*The virtue of imagination is its
reaching, by intuition and intensity
of gaze (not by reasoning) a
more essential truth than is seen
at the surface of things.*
      RUSKIN

Alas—it was not be be. Christianity swept in like a storm that carried men before it like fragile leaves and for a thousand years the world would be gripped in religious fervor; shaken to its foundation; reshaped and the powers and talents of Man made subordinate to the will of ecclesiastical power.

Kings would tremble on their thrones at the threat of excommunication; thousands of innocent people would be torn, tortured, hanged and burned in the name of goodness and mercy. Great crusades would be mounted and launched against the heretics of the Eastern world.

Once the barbarians had been thrust beyond the borders and the world settled down, the Renaissance would come into being, with a flowering of the Arts and there would be concentration on playing rather than upon serious thought or reasoning.

Just when it appeared that things were settling down and the stage was set for a rebirth of philosophical thought—*science* and *technology* moved swiftly into the scene and material inventiveness became the dominant theme of Man.

Thought was subordinated to the mathematical approach to truth. Calculating machines were rapidly replacing the independent thinker. Measurement was the key to truth. More and more intricate, complex equipment was needed. Men lent their minds to the creation of things and you began to wonder how you had ever allowed it to happen.

Man was rapidly becoming the servant of the machine. With each passing day Man's role in the scheme of things became less important. Man—it was decided was too slow—his reflexes were not on a par with the nanosecond activity of the computer. He no longer 'flew' airplanes—they were too complex—flew too fast. Man became a 'caretaker' who merely sat behind the array of instruments which—guided by a computer—performed all the complex tasks 'beyond' Man.

Your bruised ego began to suffer with all sorts of 'neurosis'—with aberrations—depressions—and, in your bewildered and unhappy state of mind, you forgot that you were actually 'free' at long last to return to your original quest.

Let the machines take over the material world—it's not really any concern of yours. What you have been seeking is not here—but there—out there in that other dimension.

The other dimension that you have been visiting for 100,000 years every night you dream.

Cogito ergo sum. You think, therefore you are.

You are not an ape. You are capable of thinking—of understanding the nature of this universe. You have the power and the means of gaining full knowledge of that 'other' world now—before you actually 'die.'

There is a bridge to that other world. It's deep inside your brain. You have used it, down through the ages, right up to this present moment, but you can't remember it. Not just yet. But you will because I'm going to *make* you remember—not just the bridge—but something more—something even more important than the bridge.

The bridge is there. It will not go away. What is more important is that you must remember *using* that bridge.

You will remember it because there is a way for you to remember. A way for you to remember everything that has happened to you in the past 100,000 years.

Just remember *this*: when I tell you that you have lived before—that you have appeared and reappeared on this Earth—again and again—down through the ages I am not just indulging in poetic license.

Think—for a moment—about yourself. About *you*. Who are you? What are you? Where did you come from?

You are the *first* born—the first created being in this world. You have died and been reborn—died and been reborn—over and over for 100,000 years *and you know that this is true because you have always suspected it almost from the time you could think!*

How many times in your life have you suddenly had a *shock of recognition* when you viewed something that was incredibly old? Some ancient statue—some monument—or when you have seen a picture of someone from another age—or when you have seen some tool or artifact that came from a civilization that disappeared a thousand years ago. You have *remembered*—for a split second and then—quickly dismissed the thought as being ridiculous. Just nonsense—how could I possibly imagine something like that? *You didn't imagine it.*

You know that I'm telling you the truth. You have never told anyone about those 'shocks' of recognition. *How could I possibly know that something like that had happened to you?*

There is a universal truth.

When General Patton stood at that ancient battleground and said, "I was *here!*" He was absolutely right. He was there—a thousand years ago.

If you visited more countries—ancient ruins—you too would suddenly be aware that you were there—a thousand years ago—a thousand lifetimes ago.

You have lived before and you will live again. More lives than you can possibly imagine are waiting for you. Each time you live—you will learn more—grow more—progress more—until that moment, somewhere in the future when you will *be*, at *one* time, in *one* place and—at the *same* time—in *all* places and *all* times forever.

201

Then you will know and understand everything.

Do you realize that you now have the power in your hands to command yourself to remember *everything?* Everything means everything since you first *stared* from the mists of the forest and realized that you could 'see' in a new and peculiar way, 100,000 years ago. Everything means that you can trace your steps forward in Time from that moment to this.

It also means that you can go forward in Time.

You now have the power to command your mind to open the portal in your mind and move through it into the other dimension that lies on the other side.

Can you think of a more exciting prospect?

The answer to everything you have been looking for lies just beyond that portal in your brain.

All you have to do is—*do it!*

How do I *know* that you can do it?

Because thousands of people are doing it at this very moment. I have been doing it since I was old enough to remember. I didn't know there was anything special about it. I just assumed that everyone did it. Then when I found out that everyone didn't do it—that people had no idea of what I was talking about—I stopped talking about it—out of *fear*. Not fear of what I was doing but fear that someone would *find out that I was doing it.*

Because of that fear I lost the ability for many years until I was much older and discovered that there *were* others who took that 'long voyage home' every night.

You will meet them when you become a 'traveler in Time' because that's what you will become. That's what it's all about in the final analysis—*Time*.

That's the key to *understanding*.

You must stop thinking about Time as something that passes—that it has duration. It doesn't. Time is a fixed dimension. *There is no past, present and future.*

It *was*—it *is*—it *will be*—these are false premises.

Everything is only a continual, eternal NOW.

You must begin to think of Time as a gigantic *maze* or *labyrinth*—a confusing network of *paths*. There is only one path that leads to the *true* exit.

All the other paths have sudden endings.

You must have—at one time or another—tried to solve one of the maze puzzles that appear quite frequently in newspapers and magazines. Do you remember, when you reached a dead end, you went back to the beginning and tried a different path? Finally—after many failures—after arriving at a host of 'dead-ends' you finally found the 'right' path and followed it through to the true exit.

Remember the sense of relief, achievement and deep satisfaction? That was a tiny reflection of 'truth' because you were 'playing' a game that closely resembles 'life'.

You are 'born' at the beginning of a path and you begin to follow it. Suddenly you come to a point where there is a choice of paths in several directions. Which way to go? If you choose 'correctly' you will continue on the path.

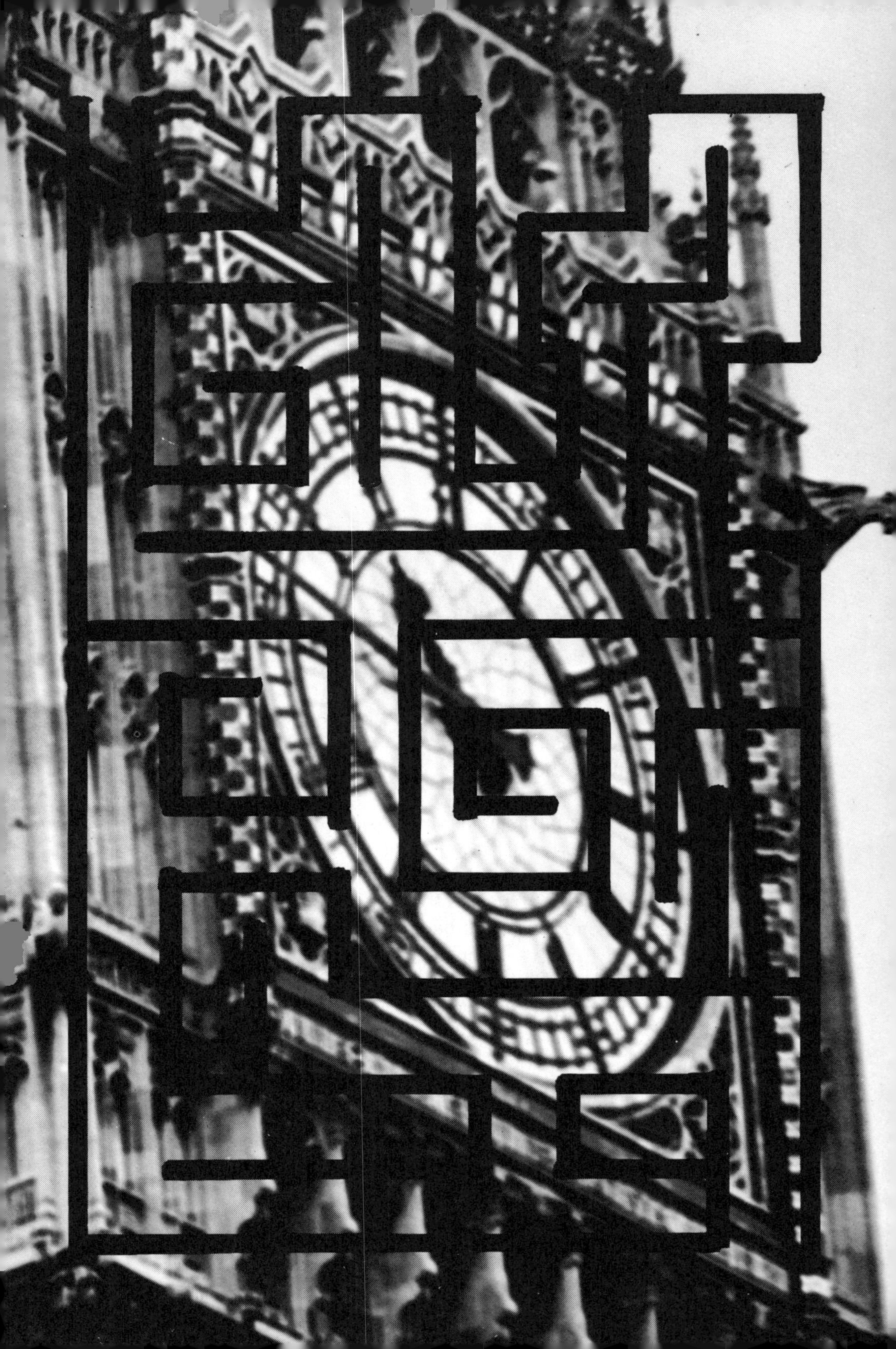

The soul in sleep gives proofs of its divine nature; for when free and disengaged from service of the body, it has a foresight of things to come whence we may conceive what will be its state when entirely freed of this bodily prison.
CICERO

If you choose 'incorrectly' you come to a 'dead-end' and you 'die'—*and then you go back to the beginning and start all over again.*

You have been doing this for 100,000 years.

Each time you were born and started on the path, there was no turning back. You had to continue moving *forward* and it was this continuous motion which gave you the idea that there was a 'past' (behind you) a 'present' (where you are now) and a 'future' (where you will be).

The maze of Time is a fixed, eternal entity. You are the *captive* of the maze from the moment that you enter it. Your *body* is bound by the laws that govern this maze.

Your *mind* is not. Your mind can rise above the maze and view it as a total structure. Your mind enables you to see the true entrance and the true exit. You can see, at one time, all the false paths and the dead-ends for the unwary traveler.

Now, in this vantage point in the other dimension, you can view the totality of the efforts of Man (you) from the very beginning. You can actually see yourself 'blind' and helpless—hands outstretched—feeling your way through 'false' paths—again and again—only to stumble finally into sudden 'death'.

You can 'see' and understand why great and powerful 'civilizations' have crumbled suddenly and mysteriously into heaps of dusty rubble.

You will see and understand something else. For the first time you will begin to realize that this great maze of Time is only the *first* of many planes of existence.

This 'present' existence is only the *kindergarten* of existence. Your graduation from this level will enable you to enter the next, *higher* level of existence.

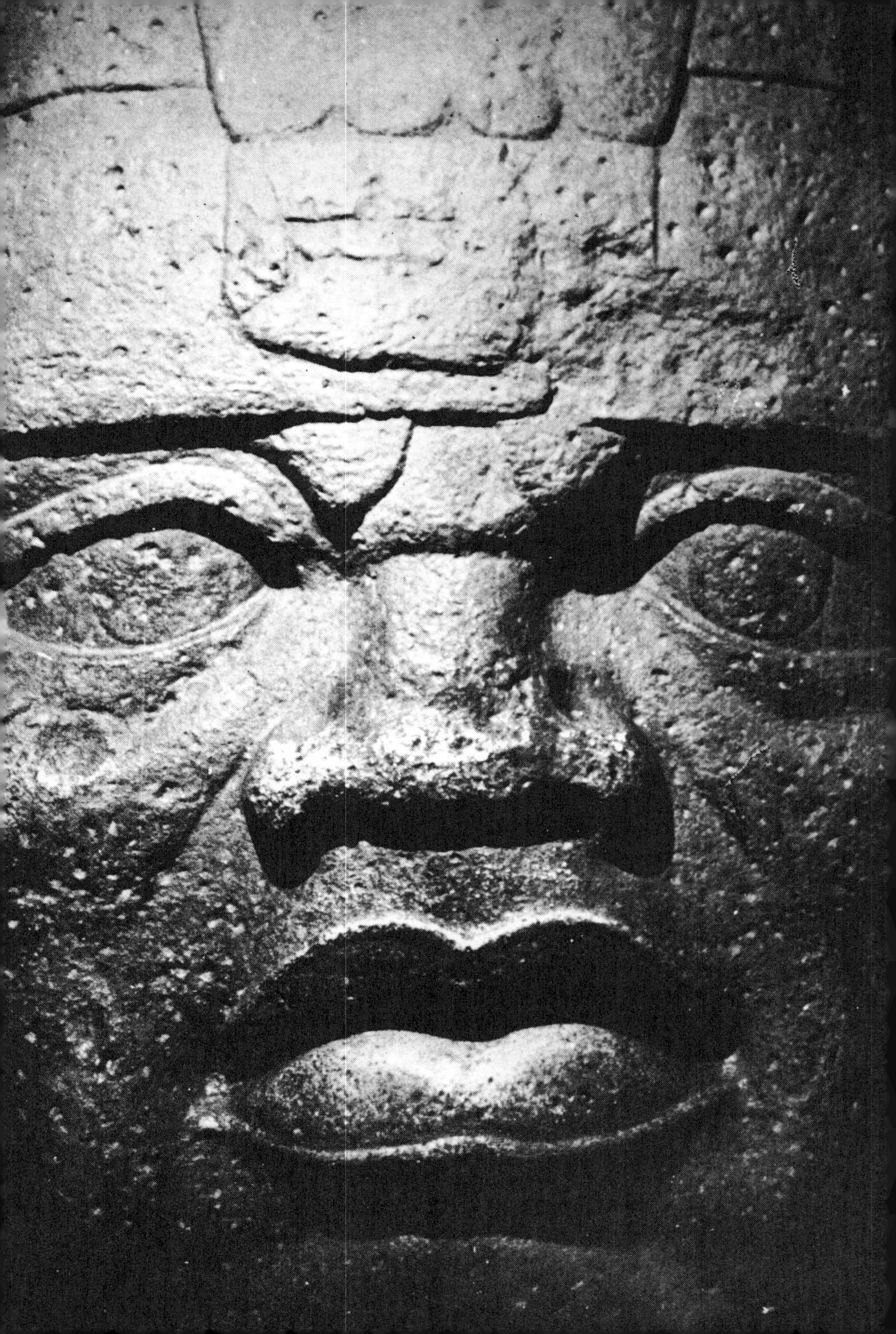

*Man cannot make a
worm, yet he can make
gods by the dozens.*
   DE MONTAIGNE

You can understand, from this vantage point, the futility of suicide. It is *not* an escape. It solves nothing. It causes pain and anguish to those who are left behind but it plunges the suicide into a dimension that can only be described as 'hellish' and—in the end—the suicide is forced to go back and start over again—no wiser than before the futile self-destruction.

You will also understand the wisdom expressed by Edgar Cayce in his description of the 'karmic law'. Each life you live *does* have a bearing on the following life. If you had beauty in a past life and misused it you will *not* have beauty in the following life. If you were cruel to others in a past life, then cruelty will be visited upon you in the following life.

"As ye sow—so shall ye reap."

It isn't easy to live a perfect life—that's why you are given so many lifetimes. The effort to live in truth and in a manner that brings no harm but rather enriches the lives of others— that is important. That moves you forward. Riches piled up in this life will have a negative effect in the following life because you are not here to become a slave to *material* things. You are here to enrich the spirit—not the substance. The substance is only illusion—the spirit is real.

Now you can appreciate the deeper meaning in the message from St. Matthew:

Wide is the gate, and broad the way, that leadeth to destruction, and many there be that go in thereat. Strait is the gate, and narrow the way, which leadeth unto Life, and few there be that find it.

The skill that you have developed—the ability to give yourself post-hypnotic suggestions—will provide you with the power to enter the *first* of the other dimensions behind this dimension.

You will, once you have entered this 'other' dimension be able to 'see' this plane of existence as it actually is. You may not stay *here*—on this plane—for long because it is extremely difficult and very fatiguing. You must move upward—to a higher plane—where you will find that you can move easily and without fatigue.

You will have many remarkable encounters but you need have no fear. You will not be alone. Others have gone before you. There will be others traveling at the same time you are. There are other 'minds' waiting to help you if you should need help. You will not have to call upon them for help.

Those older, wiser 'minds' will be aware that you have arrived at the very moment that you do arrive. They will help you if you falter; comfort you if you are fearful; assist you if you become 'lost'.

You have nothing to fear. You will have the 'key' to return to this plane at any desired moment. You only have to 'will' yourself to return and you will be back in your physical body.

It's up to you now. You have the means to make that long journey into the after-life. You have the means to learn all of the secrets of the universe if you so wish. You have the means to learn the true meaning of 'life' and the ultimate answer to the question:

WHAT HAPPENS AFTER DEATH?

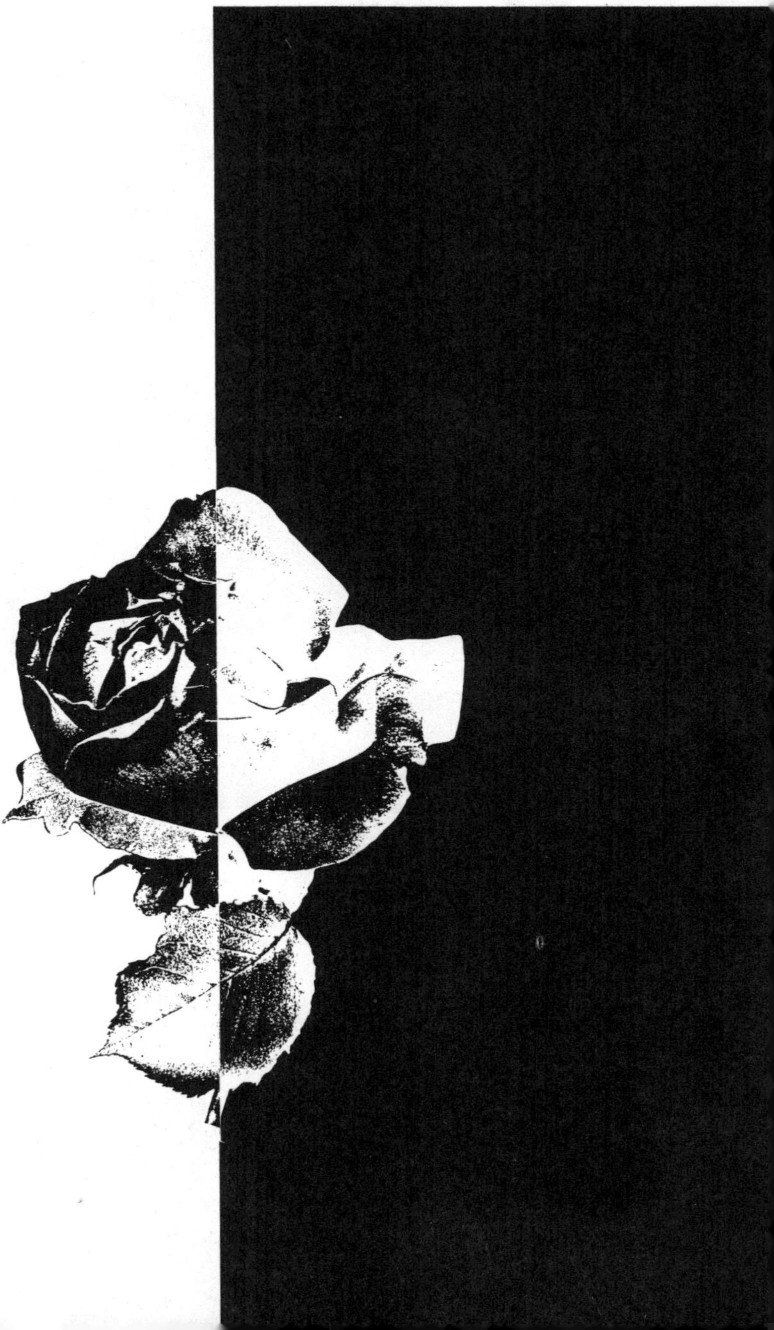

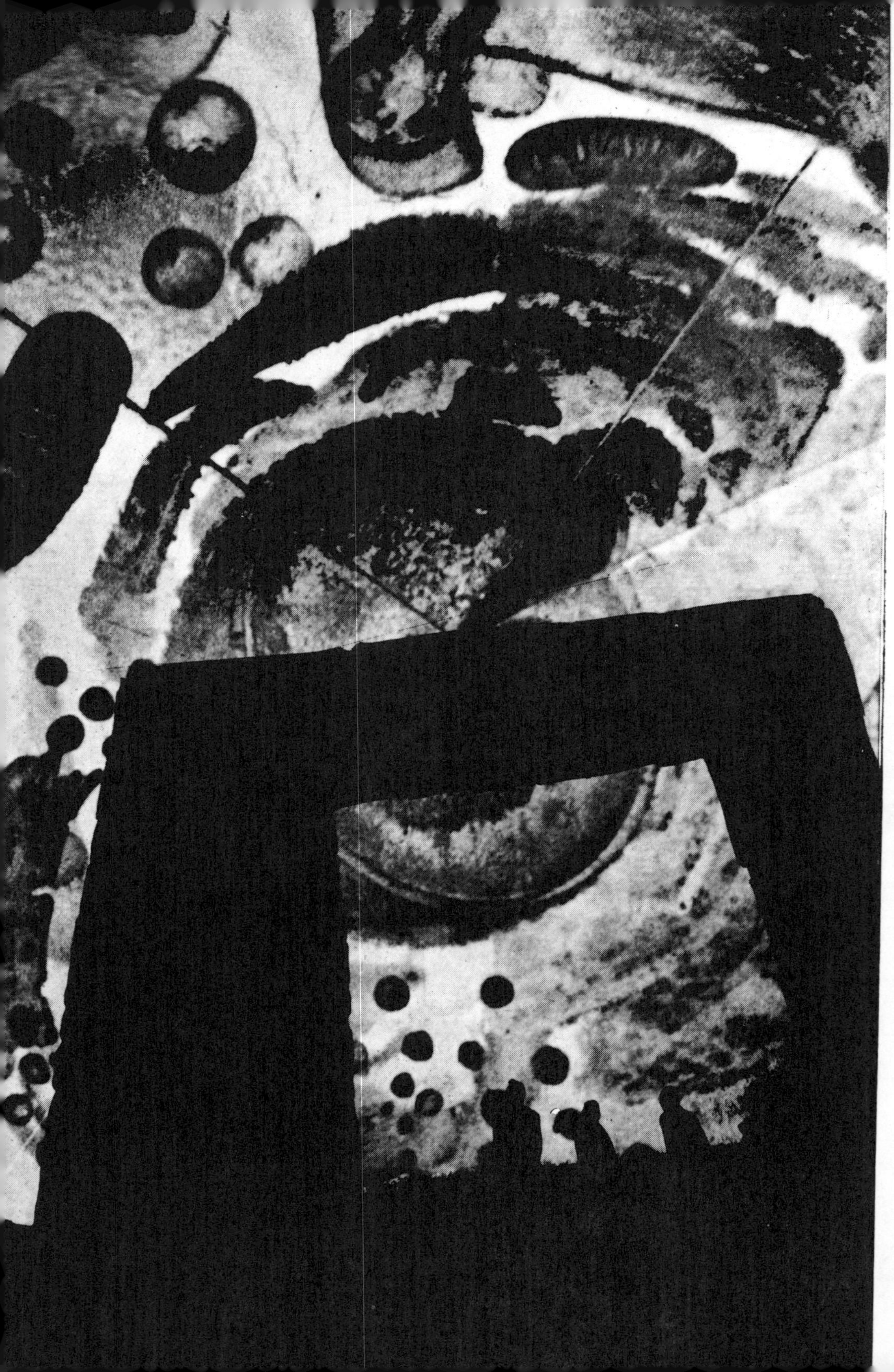

conclusion

Ladies and gentlemen of the jury we have concluded our presentation and all that remains is the summing up. In the preceding pages my associate and I have placed before you a substantial body of evidence relative to the question:
What happens after death?

It was necessary to present this kind of evidence in a particular manner and sequence because we were faced with an apparently solid wall of 'scientific' fact. Only by exposing, step-by-step, the flaws in that solid wall, could we hope to obtain an objective examination of our statements.

We began with an examination of the current theory of the origin of Life on this planet and the ultimate emergence of Mankind. This was both logical and necessary because we firmly believe that this 'scientific' theory leans too heavily on the 'accidental' and totally ignores the possibility of a prime cause of Life as well as a creator of Mankind. We have not approached this question as religious fundamentalists but rather as investigators seeking the truth instead of seeking 'facts' to support a particular theory of Life's origins.

In most instances we asked questions rather than make sweeping statements. They were reasonable questions. Is it unreasonable to question the validity of answers like 'coincidence' or 'accidental' when we ask why certain things happen? Scientists apparently expect us to accept those dubious answers because they are considered to be 'authority' figures and their word must be accepted as 'law'. In other words we are expected to place our faith in their statements blindly and without question. We are to ignore all evidence of our senses and of our minds and believe only what they tell us to believe. We are to ignore all happenings which they say did not happen. If you see something happen when you are alone then that is termed 'simple hallucination'; if there are friends and neighbors with you and they see the same thing that is called 'mass hallucination'.

While it may be easy to intimidate people with this tactic it is virtually impossible to intimidate or hide truth. The truth, as we pointed out in the Developmental Theory of Life, is that the majority of people in this world believe in the existence of a Prime Cause (or God).

We also pointed to the universal belief in a life after death.

Then we took the question of death. This is, as we said, both a simple and a complex subject. It is simple because there is no question but that it does occur. It's complex because we are still unable to accept it as a perfectly natural event. In fact, as we pointed out, we always treat 'death' as something that happens to someone else. We discussed the difference between a personal death and a physical death.

This brought us to the question of reincarnation the belief in successive lives that has persisted almost since the advent of Man. This belief has pervaded every society, every civilization throughout history.

However there was no clear evidence to support this belief until the advent of Edgar Cayce. This unique person was able to leave his body, while in an hypnotic trance, and enter another person's body for the purpose of diagnosing the cause of a particular illness or disease.

This unique ability has been fully documented and authenticated by medical authorities. While it is highly significant, we were more concerned with another aspect of this unusual talent. That is the ability to enter into and then trace back any individual's previous lives.

Cayce was most interested in the 'karmic' effect that had been created by the individual during the living of successive lives. He believed that the manner in which any individual lived had a direct bearing on the life that followed. In other words every individual who attempts to live a decent, generous and productive life will be amply rewarded in successive lifetimes whereas every individual who is selfish, greedy and hurtful will discover that a dreadful burden will be added in the next lifetime; a burden that can take many lifetimes to eliminate.

'Karmic effect' would certainly help to explain why innocent babies can be born with all sorts of physical handicaps. It would also help to explain why so many 'evil' people seem to escape the consequences of their acts while good and decent people suffer terrible harm and misfortune.

The most significant aspect of Cayce's unique talents was his unique ability to leave his body at will. He is the first to leave a documented record of thousands of out-of-body experiences (OOBE's).

We discussed this phenomenon at length in its obvious relation to death. The Tibetan Book of the Dead, for example, is a step-by-step explanation of the various stages of existence an individual passes through from the moment of 'death' to the moment of 're-birth' some 49 days later.

We also pointed to the mass of evidence which has accumulated in the past few years with regard to OOBE's. More evidence comes to light daily as more individuals find the courage to reveal experiences which previously might have caused them to be committed for mental observation.

Most recently Reader's Digest published a condensation of Doctor Raymond Moody's remarkable book—"Life After Life" which is a careful, sober presentation of documented case histories of people who were declared clinically dead.

Dr. Elizabeth Kubler-Ross, who is quite possibly the world's leading authority on death and dying, not only endorsed Dr. Raymond Moody's book—she also wrote the foreword to it.

We could have completed our book, at this point and felt that we had satisfied the reader with a valid answer to the question of what happens after death.

We didn't stop because we felt there was much more to the question than a simple affirmation of the theory of reincarnation. We believed that you wanted to know exactly how Man came into being.

Towards that end we presented certain evidence relative to the 'visible/invisible' world that surrounds us. We also asked the perfectly reasonable question as to why so many billions of dollars were being spent on investigating the known world and nothing was being spent in investigating the invisible world.

We conducted, with you, experiments in understanding the nature of dimensional 'blindness' in relation to the dimensional differences between our world and the others.

We took up the question of why people did not remember previous lives and then presented evidence that many people, including General Patton, did remember.

We discussed, at length, the phenomenon of OOBE's and gave some personal experiences with people who had OOBE's.

In our excursion, with you, into the psychic world we covered a span of time that encompassed some 50,000 years of Man's involvement with this strange world beyond this one. We pointed to the power achieved by individuals who made the journey to that other world and returned.

We showed how that power corrupted the shamans, the witch-doctors and the ancient priests and inevitably led to the advent of the god-kings of Egypt and Babylonia.

We also showed that some individuals gained the power and still remained incorruptible and tried to give the power to Man. Amenhotep IV the 'heretic' pharaoh; Gautama, the founder of Buddhism and Jesus of Nazareth all had the power and tried to give it to the people.

That they did not succeed is evidenced by the condition of the world we currently live in.

We also showed a partial list of the most famous people in history who attested to personal psychic experiences.

Our next question dealt with the strong possibility that our Earth had, in the distant past, received 'visitors' from outer space. We discussed and presented the evidence unearthed by Erich von Daniken in his several books (Chariots Of The Gods?, Gods From Outer Space, Gold Of The Gods) and Roger K. Temple's book, "The Sirius Mystery" about the Dogons of Mali. In all of these books there is solid, concrete, physical evidence of works and knowledge beyond the capacity of the residents of this Earth. We discussed the impossibility of building structures like the pyramids of Egypt and Mexico with the primitive technology of ancient Egypt and Mexico. Yet they were built by someone.

We presented evidence to show that the sudden enlargement and capability of the brain of Early Stone Age Man could not have been a result of evolution but could have been the result of intervention by the same beings who created the ancient gigantic works on Earth.
We investigated magic and religion with you and discussed the reasons why mythology is a universal language.

We showed the evidence of the vast magical work of Early Stone Age Man that has resided for 40 thousand years in the caves of Arieges in France; the significance of the labyrinths the implication of ceremonial re-birth and/or reincarnation.

Then, in order to enable you to gain deeper understanding of yourself and to help you towards an independent investigation of out-of-body experiences, we entered the world of dreams with you.

Here we discussed the various ancient and modern theories with regard to the phenomenon of dreams. We presented a practical method of remembering, reporting and interpreting your dreams. We discussed the nature of symbols and the flaw in the theory of sexual symbols.

Finally, we took you on a journey of re-discovery. We attempted to show you, in general, the many lives you have lived since the beginning of civilization. We hope that we have succeeded in revealing to you what a magnificent-creation you really are and that you are not—nor ever were—an ape.

If you believe—as we believe—that the evidence we have presented clearly demonstrates that there is indeed a life beyond this one then clearly, ladies and gentlemen of the jury—
the best is yet to come.

These new books can

MENTAL CALISTHENICS

Here's an exciting book that offers you a 30 day How-To Program of mental exercises that combine the techniques of meditation, yoga, psychoanalysis, primal, transactional analysis, written in swift-reading language. Steven West, the well known psychologist and author gives you step-by-step instruction in this easy-to-read book. **$9.95**

- Learn How To Use The Alpha Dimension
- Understanding Your Strengths And Weakness
- Learn How To Use Body Language
- Understand How To Change Your Programming
- Learn How To Eliminate Bad Habits Easily
- Understand How To Approach Sex Positively

BONUS: Long Playing Record That Teaches You How To Use The Alpha Dimension.

HOW TO LIVE LIKE A MILLIONAIRE ON AN ORDINARY INCOME

Now, for the first time, a real millionaire reveals exactly how you can live like a millionaire on an ordinary income. He tells you how he did it and then went on to really earn several million dollars! Here, in one volume, is knowledge it would take you a lifetime to accumulate. Step-by-step ways to have the life you've always wanted — and more! **$9.95**

- Brand New Luxury Cars Absolutely Free!
- Furnished Executive Suites For Nothing!
- Luxurious Dream Homes Without Any Cash!
- All Expense Vacations Absolutely Free!
- Bank Accounts Of More Than $100,000.00!
- Any Man Or Woman To Like And Admire You!
- Widespread Celebrity Status In A Week!

BONUS: Millionaire Image Building Kit Included

Your tape player can become a learning machine

HOW TO STOP SMOKING IN 30 DAYS

Here's a complete, step-by-step program on a cassette that you can play on your cassette player and learn how to stop smoking swiftly, simply, easily. This new program uses a combination of mental exercises, meditation and behavior modification that will release you from your smoking habit in 30 days time! **$9.95**

- You'll Feel Better, Look Better, Live Longer!
- You Will Not Gain Weight With This Program!
- Your Smoker's Cough Will Disappear Forever!
- You Won't Feel Frustrated Or Strung Out!
- You'll Breathe Easier, Sleep Better!

NEW PERMANENT WEIGHT LOSS PROGRAM

Now, for the first time, here's a program that you can play on your cassette player that will teach you how to lose weight easily, swiftly, permanently! Steven West, a leading psychologist and author combines the techniques of meditation, psychology and nutrition in a new, permanent, weight loss program that you can use immediately. **$9.95**

- Quick Results With Weight Loss Of 3 to 4 Pounds Each Week You Continue This Program!
- This Is An Easy Program — No Complicated Calorie Counting Or Expensive Time Consuming Gadgets!
- Improve Your Health At The Same Time You Begin To Look Better, Feel Bettery Day By Day!
- Gain New Energy, New Relaxation, Find A New Zest For Life And A Better Outlook On Life!

change your life!...

HOW TO LIVE TO BE 100 AND ENJOY IT!

There is a way for you to add 30-40 or 50 happy, vigorous, healthy years to your life span! This book tells you how to live better now and in the years to come. It offers you a complete, detailed program that you can put into operation immediately so that in less than 30 days you can start to look and feel years younger! **$9.95**

- Understand the RNA-DNA — No Aging Diet
- How To Conquer Your Dangerous Tensions
- Life Force and the 17 Rare Live Foods
- Sexuality and Alpha Waves Expand Life
- Secrets of the Hunzas — Live to 125
- 60 Second Heart Exercise To Keep Young

BONUS: WEIGHT CONTROL SUPPLEMENT
3000 Different Foods Evaluated

THE POWER & PLEASURE OF SEX

Now you can release the passionate, uninhibited lover that's been trapped inside you all your life! Here, in a unique new book is the knowledge you have been looking for! It's a completely new and different approach to sexual relations which, will for the first time permit you to become the lover you have always wanted to be. **$9.95**

- Acting Out Your Sexual Fantasies
- Primal Sensuality Discoveries
- Getting To Know The Nude You
- Developing Your Sensual Nature
- The Art Of Self Exploration
- Writing Your Sexual Biography
- Giving/Receiving Love Massage

BONUS SUPPLEMENT: ANALYSIS OF THE KINSEY/MASTERS & JOHNSON/HITE REPORT

AMW

Aabbott McDonnell-Winchester
376 Wyandanch Avenue
North Babylon, New York 11704

Please send me the following books (cassettes) @ $9.95 each plus .95¢ ea. for postage and handling.

- ☐ Mental Calisthenics
- ☐ Live like a millionaire
- ☐ Live to be 100
- ☐ Power & pleasure of sex
- ☐ Stop smoking in 30 days
- ☐ Permanent weight loss

☐ Check enclosed   ☐ Charge my credit card;
☐ Master Charge card # _____ Exp. Date _____
☐ BankAmericard # _____ Exp. Date _____

Name _____

Address _____

New York residents add 7% sales tax.

City _____

State _____ Zip _____